KK-697
1st edition
12-

the home gardener's book of

ferns

by john mickel
with evelyn fiore

a
ridge
press
book

holt,
rinehart and
winston
new york

Editor-in-Chief: Jerry Mason
Editor: Adolph Suehsdorf
Art Director: Albert Squillace
Project Art Director: Harry Brocke
Associate Editor: Ronne Peltzman
Associate Editor: Joan Fisher
Art Associate: Nancy Mack
Art Associate: Liney Li
Art Production: Doris Mullane

Published by Holt, Rinehart and Winston, 383 Madison Avenue,
New York, New York 10017.
Published simultaneously in Canada by Holt, Rinehart and Winston
of Canada, Limited.
Prepared and produced by The Ridge Press, Inc.

Library of Congress Cataloging in Publication Data
Mickel, John.
The home gardener's book of ferns.
"A Ridge Press book."
Includes index.
1. Ferns, Ornamental. 2. Ferns. I. Fiore,
Evelyn L. II. Title.
SB429.M52   635.9′37′31   78-14418

ISBN Hardbound: 0-03-045736-X
ISBN Paperback: 0-03-045741-6
First edition
Printed in the United States of America
10   9   8   7   6   5   4   3   2   1

contents

in fact and fancy

ferns go far back into prehistory. They were not our earliest plants; that niche is occupied by the algae and bacteria, which were recognizable two billion years ago. But ferns developed hard on the algae's heels. Nearly 400 million years ago they were greening up the vast damp spaces of our still unpeopled planet, combining with horsetails, clubmosses, and the few other primitive plants to create the dense vegetation that would gradually decay into our treasure of coal deposits.

In spite of the eons behind them, ferns are not one of the larger plant orders. But being tough and resourceful, they have learned to survive in every part of the world except the coldest and most arid regions, and in the course of all this adaptation have become fascinatingly diverse. We usually think of a fern as feathery or lacy—the name itself, traceable back through the Old English *fearn* to the Sanskrit *parna*, has always meant "wing" or "feather"— yet just beyond the prototypical feathery-fronded varieties there are many surprises. The hart's-tongue and the stag's-tongue, among others, have solid, undivided leaves. There is the leathery staghorn, with its bizarre resemblance to a set of antlers. Some ferns live in water; some are epiphytic, sending out long ropelike rhizomes that twine so luxuriantly around their supporting trees that the host may be unrecognizable. In the genus *Trichomanes* there are ferns no larger than peas, while some tropical tree ferns soar to heights of 60 feet and more. Often amateur gardeners shy away from ferns, because they have a reputation for being difficult. Yet their adaptability in nature shows that many ferns can be coaxed to settle into the garden, indoors or out, by a gardener who is attentive to their needs.

what is a fern?

Plants are classified by their structure, the way they grow, and the way they reproduce, not by the way they look. (See Appendix, page 249). One of the most typically "fernlike" of plants, the airy, lacy, multifronded asparagus fern, is not a fern at all but a relative of the lily.

A fern is a green plant with the characteristic plant organs of roots, stems, and leaves, but without flowers or fruit. The roots are fine, wiry structures, dark brown with cream-colored growing tips. Like all roots, they anchor the plant to its substratum and absorb water and minerals from the soil.

This raw food material is carried through the plant by a vascular, or conducting, system. Again, this is typical of most plants as we know them. What sets ferns and the plants we call fern allies (pages 54–67) apart and gives them their intriguing link with the dawn of life on earth is that they were the first plants to struggle up out of the algal ooze and

Compression of a fossil fern from
a clay pit in Iowa. The fern is approximately
250 million years old.

11

develop this vascular system through which nourishment could be drawn up and distributed.

The conducting system is of course hidden within the plant, but it need not remain mysterious. You can get a look at it quite easily by cutting off a leaf stalk and examining the cut end under a magnifying glass. The vascular bundles will be easily distinguishable. In some stalks they are particularly easy to see because the vascular systems tend to be darker than surrounding tissue. What appears is some variety of U-shaped pattern: it may be in the form of a gutter, two strap-shaped bundles, or several small round bundles. If you work these ends loose from the stalk and carefully pull them out, you will find that far from being fragile they are tough enough to be used as string—though perhaps not for tying up anything much bigger than a breadbox.

Fern stems (rhizomes) are generally creepers. They proceed horizontally underground or along the surface of the ground, covering in their stride any rock or other obstruction that lies in their way; they may also work their way up trees and twine out along the branches. Some, like the ostrich fern, have an ascending stem that grows a crown of leaves. What is most typical of all fern stems is that they are clothed with a kind of armor of hairs or scales beneath which are concealed the plant's growing tips. This survival mechanism is all-important to the life of the fern, since the growing tip is the site of all stem growth and the initiation of all leaves, and if it were vulnerable to damage the plant would be finished.

Its leaves are the fern's major component. In fact, a fern plant is largely leaf, and this is true whether the leaves are delicate and finely divided or broad and coarse. As in other plants, the leaves are the plant's food factory. In the process

called photosynthesis, they combine water and minerals from the soil with carbon dioxide drawn from the air to form sugars and other compounds needed in the plant's metabolism. Through the vascular system, the food is transported for use or storage in other parts of the plant.

While they function like other leaves, fern leaves grow in a unique manner. In most plant groups, the leaves as they grow enlarge in all directions at once. Young fern leaves start out tightly rolled, in a shape that looks enough like a bishop's crosier, or like the head of a violin, for the names crosier and fiddlehead to have been adopted for them. But instead of spreading out uniformly as they age,

Fiddlehead of the ostrich fern (*Matteuccia struthiopteris*).

13

14

Close-up of the lower surface
of the common polypody (*Polypodium
virginianum*) showing several sori,
each with many sporangia.

they mature first at the base, then unroll gradually as maturation continues toward the tip. Botanically speaking, this method of growth is probably the fern's most distinctive feature.

Also distinctive, though not unique, is the fern's reproductive system. Lacking flowers and fruit, it does not produce seeds, which were a relatively sophisticated development in the evolution of plant life. Ferns reproduce today just as they and their companion plants did in the far-off Carboniferous period, before any flowering, fruiting, seed-bearing plants had appeared: by means of spores. These minute, one-celled structures are produced in spore cases (sporangia), and if you want to cultivate ferns, one of the first things you should do is learn to recognize these spore cases. They occur in clusters called sori, which look like brown dots on the undersides of the leaves, and an over-eager but uninformed grower is all too likely to scrape them off, mistaking them for insects or disease.

At maturity, the spores are released into the air, falling where they will. Those lucky enough to fall on moist places germinate, and in a process described in Chapter 3 go on to become a new generation.

myth, magic, and medicine

Before the eighteenth century, observers of the natural world knew nothing about spores. They were aware that some plants gave off a kind of "dust," but they never associated this with procreation. It was taken for granted that all plants reproduced by seeds, which, however tiny, could be identified. Ferns, springing up all over the world without seeds, were consequently something out of the ordinary, and they were credited with supernatural powers. Superstitions and myths grew up around them.

For instance, there was the myth of invisibility. Along with the alchemist's dream of creating gold, the power to make oneself invisible has been one of the most persistent and beguiling of human fantasies—and the fern seed must possess that power, for how else could it remain unseen and untouched while fern plants went on proliferating? It followed that anyone who managed to come into possession of a fern seed would also control the magic and be able to make himself invisible at will. Even Shakespeare noted the superstition, though mockingly, in *Henry IV*: "We have the receipt of fernseed, we walk invisible."

This belief was in some ways an extension of the ancient medical theory called the Doctrine of Signatures, which held that the uses of a plant or mineral were revealed in its form. Thus, yellow flowers could cure jaundice. The red-flecked bloodstone would stop a hemorrhage. As for the already mysterious fern, its applications were legion. The rounded leaflets of the moonwort were helpful in treating lunacy. If you were bitten by a snake, you sought out (if you had time) the adder's-tongue fern, whose erect, fertile spike might be said to resemble a snake's tongue. If the poet Michael Drayton (1563–1631) wasn't being satirical, he believed this along with other educated men of his time, for he wrote:

> For them that are with newts, or snakes or adders stung
> He seeketh out a herb that's called adder's-tongue,
> As nature it ordained its own like hurts to cure,
> And sportive, did herself to niceties inure.

Apart from such "medical" mythology, many magical powers were ascribed to ferns and fern allies. To put a curse on an enemy, you blew the "dust" of horsetails toward him while uttering your imprecation. The touch of the useful moonwort would open any lock; it would also unshoe horses pasturing in meadows where it grew.

One fern is still sold as a charm, or at least a tourist item, in Taiwan. This is the famous vegetable lamb of Tartary, a small woolly object with a reasonably identifiable head, tail, and legs. Actually, the lamb is the growing tip of the East Asian tree fern *Cibotium barometz*. The leaf bases form the legs, the stem is the body, and the whole is covered with the golden hairs characteristic of this plant. Its magical powers are moot, but perhaps it merits a place on the traveler's souvenir shelf, next to the South American shrunken heads.

In England in the Middle Ages the cut stalk of the bracken (*Pteridium aquilinum*) was an especially adaptable charm, and all because of the vascular bundles we have already observed. Some interpreters saw the broken-circle pattern as standing for the letter C, Christ's initial. To them, the bracken possessed good magic, providing protection against goblins. In the opposite corner were those who saw the pattern as the mark of the devil's hoof. The amorous turned it to their own purposes: it was the initial either of your loved one or of someone you would kiss before the day was over. This must have been a fruitful superstition for those named Oliver or Clara or even Gregory, but the Marys, Kenneths, and Thomases must have felt very much left out.

Bracken—perhaps because there is so much of it—had endless uses. When the king of England wished to go hunting in the countryside, farmers were ordered not to burn the bracken, for it was well known that the way to bring on rain was to set a field of bracken alight. Bracken fires would also drive out witches and similar nuisances. In 1629 John Parkinson, a sound enough naturalist for his time, explained in his herbal *Paradisi in Sole* how the smoke from the burning ferns "driveth away serpents, gnats and other noisome creatures." It isn't clear whether he realized that fire alone would do this, or was investing the smoke of the bracken with mystical superpowers. Parkinson also wrote that the "sent" of the fumes was "very gratefull to the braine." Like most of the ancient medical claims made for various ferns, this has never been supported by research. Yet a good handful of such claims persist. Science either has not altogether scotched them, or in some cases has not yet investigated them fully.

The most unimpeachable fern medical credentials belong to the male fern (*Dryopteris filix-mas*), which for hundreds of years has been employed as a vermifuge. (Does this show some relation to Parkinson's claim that burning ferns drove out "noisome creatures"?) At any rate, the male fern is still listed in current pharmacopoeias.

In Mexican markets today, the rhizomes of the golden polypody (*Polypodium aureum*) and *Lophosoria quadripinnata*, a trunkless tree fern, are sold to cure ailments of the liver, kidneys, and heart. In Costa Rica, tea brewed from the hard-to-find giant horsetail (*Equisetum giganteum*) is widely used to treat kidney diseases. So certain are the vendors of the horsetail's medical value that they try to monopolize its supply. Ask where they have found it and you will be told, with a vague gesture, "*En las montañas*" ("In the mountains").

One evergreen polypody, boiled with sugar, was much used throughout Europe as a cure for whooping cough; perhaps it still is, in some places. The West Indian *Polypodium lycopodioides* is prepared as a tea to cure colds. If you have sensitive teeth, you might try chewing on the first fern

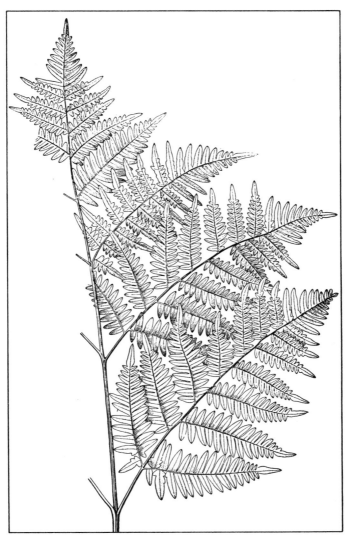

Bracken (*Pteridium aquilinum*).

19

fronds you see in the spring; somewhere this picked up a reputation as a toothache-preventive.

Waiting on research timetables are at least two serious medical possibilities. In 1854 John Smith, a fern specialist at England's Kew Gardens, described how the small fern *Anemia oblongifolia* was used in Panama to induce abortion. This claim is now being investigated. And reports from Honduras that some forms of cancer have been arrested by *Polypodium decumanum* have brought this fern under pharmaceutical scrutiny. It is a close relative of the commonly cultivated golden polypody.

fern soufflé, anyone?— and other uses

Any plant that has been around as long as the fern has naturally been checked out for its food qualifications. Many varieties are eaten in the fiddlehead stage, when the tender young leaves are just beginning to unroll. The fiddleheads of the ostrich fern (*Matteuccia struthiopteris*), one of the largest temperate-zone ferns, are so popular in northeastern North America that they are harvested by the ton and sold fresh, frozen, and canned. Relatively free of hairs and scales, with an asparaguslike flavor, they can be used in salads, served as a vegetable, added to soups, and made into soufflés. The adventurous cook will find even more suggestions in *Feasting on Fiddleheads*, a currently available book of fern recipes published by the American Fern Society.

In Korea and Japan fiddleheads of the royal fern (*Osmunda regalis*) and the bracken are dried or preserved in liquid for use as food. In Scotland bracken rhizomes are occasionally dug up and roasted. But recent medical evidence indicates that eating any part of these ferns may be a bad idea. Since 1920 stomach tumors in cattle have been associated with the animals' grazing on bracken, and recent studies confirm that this fern has carcinogenic properties. Compounds of known carcinogenic activity have been found in the royal, and in fact in the ostrich as well, but no tests have been made on animal subjects and it is not yet known whether the compounds are present in dangerous quantities.

One large fleshy fern, *Marattia weinmanniifolia*, is a valuable food in the mountains of southern Mexico. The Indians call it *maís del monte*—"mountain corn." Fleshy outgrowths, or stipules, swell on its large leaf bases and remain attached to the rhizome when the leaves fall off. They are somewhat mucilaginous and very starchy, and in times of crop failure the Indians use them as a substitute for corn, grinding them up to make tortillas.

In addition to their uses in medicinal teas, ferns and fern allies are brewed into a variety of beverages. In Europe the rhizomes of the male fern and the bracken are sometimes substituted for hops in beer-making. Wild-plant-tea enthusiasts, who will pour boiling water over anything that seems even remotely eligible, claim that the dried leaves of the maidenhair fern (*Adiantum pedatum*) make a fine tea. Its public, so far, is small. Another odd taste comes from the fine-branching stems of the common horsetail (*Equisetum arvense*), which are dried and packaged as "shave-grass tea." It does not yield a strong flavor, but from what I sampled, this is just as well.

Almost any natural material that exists in substantial quantity is used by someone, somewhere, for practical purposes. In parts of the world where ferns—particularly bracken—grow thickly, they are often used as bedding for

21

cattle, and sometimes for thatching roofs. In tropical rain forests where tree ferns reach significant size, their trunks are used in constructing houses and bridges. The trunks are generally only a few inches in diameter and do not form wood inside as do woody seed plants, but their internal conducting systems give them surprising strength. Surrounded by heavy layers of fibers, these vascular bundles provide enough rigidity and resistance to make the slender trees a very useful building material.

The stem apexes and leaf bases of some tree ferns are covered with long golden hairs, so thickly massed that they form soft nests among the leaf bases. Called *pulu* in Hawaii, the cushiony material is collected from the native tree fern *Cibotium* and used to stuff pillows.

There is a large central pith of starchy tissue in the trunks of many tree ferns. In the early years of this century an entire industry was involved in extracting and refining this pulpy mass into laundry starch.

Even the bracken that was burned to scare off witches did not entirely go up in smoke. Bracken ashes, as well as those of the male fern, were at one time used in the manufacture of glass, and in seventeenth-century China fern ashes were used in glazing pottery.

Spores, produced in such great quantity, have naturally not been overlooked. The clubmosses often bear their spores in cones at the tips of aerial branches, which are easy to collect and dry. Some of this powdery substance was used in photographic flash powder; some went into gunpowder. Fern spores are now being investigated to see if they might have similar pyrotechnic capacity. Clubmoss spores also show anticoagulant properties, and have been of medical use. They serve in a minor way as a coating on

Painting of the rabbit's-foot
fern (*Davallia fejeensis* var. *plumosa*), one
of a series by Manabu Saito.

23

24

Top: First-day cover of four fern stamps
from Guernsey, showing (left to right) a spleenwort, a
quillwort, a spleenwort, and an adder's-tongue.
Bottom: Eighteenth-century twenty-
shilling note depicting the evergreen wood fern.

pharmaceutical pills, to keep them from sticking together. We see, then, that ferns have been fairly hard-working members of the plant kingdom, not just pretty faces. But pretty faces—or, more properly, pretty forms—they certainly are, and many generations of artists have taken note of their grace and charm. They appear in numberless drawings and paintings, notably in a recent fern series by the artist Manabu Saito. The actual fronds are often used as templates from which book illustrations are printed. This technique was even used on money in the early days of the United States, when Benjamin Franklin, anxious to frustrate possible counterfeiting of the bills he was printing, used nature-printed leaves as patterns because each leaf was unique and could not be copied. The leaflet of the evergreen wood fern (*Dryopteris intermedia*) was one of his choices.

Ferns and fern allies have been reproduced on postage stamps, (the tiny Isle of Guernsey alone issued five different kinds), on fabrics, on housewares both decorative and practical. Dried fronds are made into arrangements and even into pictures, an old-fashioned craft now coming back into vogue. Pressed fronds are encased in plastic and used to make lampshades, bookmarks, and place mats; they are sometimes embedded in wax in candles. The clubmosses *Lycopodium clavatum* and *L. flabelliforme* used to be made into Christmas wreaths, and the Hartford climbing fern (*Lygodium palmatum*) was also a popular wintertime decoration, but these uses are now illegal. The species are increasingly rare and are protected by law against collection for such purposes.

2.

a vast array

fern leaves do not stop with making themselves the most conspicuous part of the plant—nearly all of it that can be seen. They also display such a rich variety of sizes and forms that Thoreau, looking around at them in his New England woods and fields, observed, "Nature made ferns for pure leaves, to show what she could do in that line." With its vast diversity, the fern world does indeed seem like a laboratory run by nature to see how many leaf variations it can come up with.

However, while the leaves are what we see, the overall shape or "habit" of the plant is really controlled by the way in which its stem, or rhizome, grows, and the rhizomes seem to share to some extent the nonconformist tendencies of the leaves. They don't display as much diversity, but they do work their way along in quite a few different ways.

rhizomes: shape, size, and habit

In most ferns the rhizome creeps horizontally along, or just beneath, the soil surface, sometimes branching, sometimes developing into a clump. If the rhizome is short-creeping the clump is compact; leaves go up in all directions, reflecting the several directions of the growing tips. If the rhizome is long-creeping, with spaces between the fronds, the clump can become so large that it sprawls over a whole hillside or meadow, often crowding out other plant life. To be blunt about it, some of these aggressive ferns can be weeds. Bracken is the most notorious of these spreaders, so persistent and far-ranging that it has sometimes been suggested in jest that all the bracken in the world must really be a single plant.

Top: The spreading crowns
of the ostrich fern. Bottom: The
long-creeping rhizome of the bramble
fern (*Hypolepis repens*).

29

Most rhizomes grow very slowly, remaining close to the soil until the stem tip, or crown, takes a characteristic upward curve. Leaves grow from this crown to form a plant that is frequently vase-shaped, a shape especially noticeable in the holly ferns (*Polystichum*), the wood ferns (*Dryopteris*), and the ostrich ferns (*Matteuccia*).

Less commonly, the rhizome becomes a climber. In some species, if the rhizome encounters a tree as it feels its way along the ground, the fern goes up instead of going around. It hangs on to the tree with its roots, drawing support, water, and minerals from the bark. These climbers often have spectacular leaves. The stout, scaly rhizome of *Polybotrya* produces leaves that spread up to 4 feet outward from the trunk. The widely cultivated *Stenochleana* has a long, slender rhizome so nearly naked that it resembles a tough green rope as it twists up the trunk of its host tree and festoons the branches with its widely spaced, coarse, once-divided leaves.

The greatest diversity of stem forms is probably found in the genus *Blechnum*. *Blechnum fragile* and *B. ensiforme* are climbers, their aggregated (densely massed) leaves erupting in a single whorl on the trunk of a tree. But other *Blechnums* are short-creeping, long-creeping, slightly ascending; some are tree ferns, with fully erect stout trunks that need no support (these, however, are unrelated to the other tree ferns).

Ferns with treelike forms—tree ferns—are strikingly graceful, with slender trunks crowned with tufts of long, gently arching dissected fronds and occasional crosiers. Mexicans call them *rabo de león*—"lion's tail." Generally they are found in forests, since they are shallow-rooted and easily blown over in the open. They range in height from a few

A 60-foot tree fern
(*Sphaeropteris horrida*) towers over its neighbors
in a rain forest in southern Mexico.

31

feet to 60 feet, which is remarkable, since the trunks are typically only 3 to 6 inches in diameter and have no woody growth to aid in their support. Their strength comes from their vascular bundles, which are thick, tough, and reinforced by protective sheaths of dense fibers. Some are further secured by dense masses of aboveground roots that mantle the trunk, helping to nourish as well as to support.

fronds: nature's leaf laboratory

Anyone who spends any time at all looking at ferns soon learns better, but many people still think of a "fernlike" leaf as many times divided, finely cut, lacy. To be sure, there are many multidivided ferns. The most finely cut are actually five times dissected, or divided. But many are only once-divided, and many display gradations between the extremes. It is these variations in dissection, plus the multitude of differences in frond shape, texture, and shading, that make it seem as though the fern world is totally occupied by delicately frothy shapes, with no two species alike.

Actually, there are even many ferns with undivided, or simple, leaves. Often these are broad ribbons with their own kind of grace, like the leaves of the strap ferns of tropical America (*Polypodium* subgenus *Campyloneuron*) and the various "tongue" ferns: hart's-tongue (*Phyllitis*), adder's-tongue (*Ophioglossum*), and stag's-tongue (*Elaphoglossum*). Or they may go to the other extreme, as in the shoestring fern (*Vittaria*), which has fronds only about an eighth of an inch wide. This epiphyte flourishes in wet tropical forests, hanging from tree trunks and branches like clusters of strings—most unfernlike.

There are also relatively undivided ferns with short, broad, deep-lobed fronds. The strawberry fern (*Hemionitis*) and the hand fern (*Doryopteris*) are two whose leaves develop interesting star and arrowhead shapes. Handsome and easily cultivated, they make fine terrarium plants. Some ferns have kidney-shaped leaves. Two worth searching out are the kidney maidenhair (*Adiantum reniforme*) and the Chinese kidney fern (*Sinephropteris delavayi*). The latter has been neglected, for what mysterious reason I do not know; it is an attractive plant that would certainly do well in cultivation.

Within the broad outlines of frond width and dissection, there are further refinements that add even more variety. Most fronds are pinnately divided, that is, the frond is constructed like a feather, with the leaflets, or pinnae, all coming off a central shaft, which is called the rachis (pronounced *ray*-kiss). The leaflets, if they are divided, follow the same feather pattern, with the pinnules, or segments, coming off both sides of the pinnae. A variation of this pattern is found in ferns in which the bottom segments of the lowest pair of pinnae are greatly exaggerated, making the base of each pinna much wider than the top. The frond then becomes star-shaped or hand-shaped. When the frond is much divided, it may appear to be five-sided, as in *Pteris quadriaurita*. The most complex of these is *Pteris podophylla*, in which the lowest pair of pinnae are as large as the whole rest of the frond. The lowest pinnule on each pair of basal pinnae is also highly exaggerated, becoming nearly as large as the "parent" pinna and giving rise to a large basal segment. The end result is a frond whose architecture is nearly semicircular. Visualize these complex objects growing to heights of 8 to 12 feet—for this is what they do—and you'll have some idea of the spectacular sight they make in their native tropical rain forests.

33

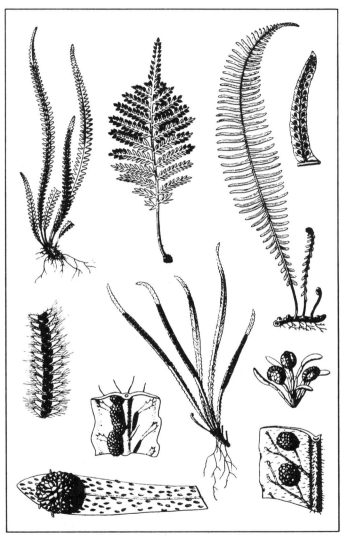

One of the beauties of
ferns is their apparently endless diversity
of frond form, ranging
from undivided to finely cut.

35

Forking Ferns. In many ferns an unexpected forking occurs at the tips of the fronds. This condition, called cresting, is actually an abnormality that suddenly shows itself in an individual plant. Occasionally the plant transmits it genetically to its offspring. Some genetic oddities in botany are quickly squelched, but crested fern species are prized because they are interesting, beautiful, and add new possibilities. In the cloud forests of Costa Rica there grows the most highly crested fern I have seen in the wild, *Grammitis fucoides*. Up to now it has not been successfully cultivated, but specialists are continuing their attempts, because with its pinnae forking repeatedly to become as large as the rest of the frond, this fern is an extraordinary specimen.

We do have in captivity one of the most dramatic of forking ferns—the staghorn, of the genus *Platycerium*. The fronds of this curious specimen fork consistently, in some cases as many as four times; it is this forking factor that creates the antlered look so appealing to many plant-lovers. The bizarre antlers are true spotlight-grabbers, eclipsing the interesting fact that the staghorn also produces a set of so-called shield leaves—broad, cabbagelike leaves that modestly hug the tree on which the plant grows in the wild or the plaque on which it is displayed in the living room, protecting the stem and roots, trapping moisture, and providing nutrients.

Drynarias, like the oak-leaf fern (*Drynaria quercifolia*), also grow two kinds of leaves. The large ones produce spores and food and then fall off, leaving behind on the rhizome a set of smaller ones that look somewhat like erect oak leaves.

Climbing Ferns. Most fern fronds follow a typical growth pattern. The leaves unroll from base to tip, and when the frond reaches its genetically dictated mature size, it stops growing. But there are a maverick few—the so-called climbing ferns—that seem willing to go on indefinitely. The most widely known of these is *Lygodium*. Its fifty species are mostly tropical, but one is native to the eastern United States.

The *Lygodium* stem is a short-creeping rhizome in the soil, which sends up slender, vinelike fronds. The rachis twines on any contacting object, climbing as much as 30 feet and entangling itself energetically with any growing things within reach. Long before the leaf tip has finished unrolling, the lower pinnae have matured and released their spores. *Lygodium* makes a fairly reliable house plant, and its odd growth habit makes it an interesting one. There are several species in cultivation.

The longest frond in the world, by present knowledge, belongs to *Salpichlaena volubilis*. The rhizome creeps in the ground, sending up twice-cut fronds that are perfectly capable of climbing 50 feet into the surrounding trees. Not quite in the same league is the genus *Hypolepis*, but while it doesn't match *Salpichlaena* in length it does go on growing for very prolonged periods. Interesting, too, is that this relative of the bracken grows in a peculiar on-and-off fashion. The crosier unrolls to produce a pair of pinnae, then stops unrolling while the pinnae mature. The pinnae having done their thing, the crosier takes over again, unrolling to release another pair of pinnae. The plant goes on in this way to make a frond 20 or so feet long that leans on any surrounding vegetation it can reach.

There is an ancient forking-fern group, the genus *Gleichenia* and its relatives, that grows in a similar manner. The leaves arise from an underground rhizome, and as the cro-

sier stops unrolling, a single pair of pinnae is produced directly under its apex. The crosier, in this group, does not resume growth. It is the pinnae that go on to fork, their coiled apexes in turn becoming dormant. Different forking patterns are produced by different species, but the growing blueprint remains the same—always a series of dormant apexes flanked by a pair of pinnae. The fronds are likely to grow many feet long, and since the long-creeping rhizomes

The fronds of the forking fern (*Gleichenia bifida*) divide at the tip.

This filmy fern (*Trichomanes curtii*) is less than a half-inch wide and only one cell thick.

39

produce many fronds, there is almost no such thing as a single *Gleichenia* or even a small grouping. What you're likely to get is an extensive thicket. Like the bracken, this is a takeover plant that needs to be watched when it commences invasion procedures.

At the opposite end of the frond size range are the filmy ferns of the genera *Trichomanes* and *Hymenophyllum*. The average fern fancier rarely gets the chance to become familiar with these. Not only do they hide in dark forests, cowering among mosses and liverworts; many are minute as well, about the size of the nail of your little finger. If you went exploring with an experienced botanist in the forests of Central America you might get a look at *Trichomanes godmanii*, one of the smallest, because it pretty consistently grows on the bases of palm trees. Your guide would know just where to bend over and peer in order to spot it. Such moments of discovery are among the thrills of botany; unfortunately, it's mostly the professionals who get to experience them.

Texture.   Just as fern fronds differ from one another in form, size, habit, and other characteristics, they differ in texture, too. Many are so thin—even translucent—that they dry out easily, supporting the rumor that all ferns are nothing but trouble for the indoor gardener. Not so. Many, because their thinness prevents them from retaining moisture, do indeed need high humidity—higher than our living quarters offer unless special care is taken. The delicate filmy ferns are only one cell thick and require a relative humidity of almost 100 percent. But there are other ferns that are not so thin-textured, with firm and leathery leaves that give them excellent prospects for survival indoors. Some are so leathery that the details of their vein patterns can't be seen

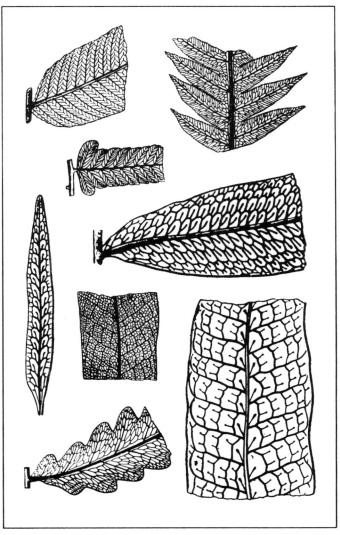

Diversity of vein patterns in ferns.
Although most ferns have free (not uniting)
veins, as seen at upper left, many
have distinctive forms of vein networks.

even when they are held up against a strong light. A number of these thick leaves tend to be dull-surfaced, which makes them perhaps a little less desirable for an indoor garden, but the bird's-nest and several others boast an attractive sheen.

Venation. When you become intimate enough with your ferns to study their venation (vein systems) you discover a rich new source of interest. Their vein patterns are marvelously diverse, and as eye-catching as many a modern painting.

Most ferns have what are called free veins: each runs from the midvein to the leaf margin without uniting with other veins to form a network. Some species can be identified solely on the basis of their vein design—whether or not the veins fork, and whether the forking occurs at the vein base or elsewhere along its path. But it is in the net-veined forms that the patterns become most inventively complex.

protection: hairs and scales

The hairs or scales that so effectively protect the rhizome are found on the rest of the plant as well. They are most heavily concentrated on the stem apex, the plant's growing tip, but the fronds also often show a thin coat. Since they are fairly distinctive for particular groups of ferns, these coverings can be helpful in identification. It's a good idea, therefore, to learn to distinguish hairs from scales, and to recognize the different types of each that occur.

Structures that are only a single cell wide, and one to many cells long, are generally considered hairs. A structure two or more cells wide is a scale. To be sure, this is an arbitrary distinction, and there are transitional forms in between, but for the most part the thin hairs can easily be distinguished from the broader scales. The covering that appears on leaves is usually hairy rather than scaly. On the rhizome, however, hairs are found only in the more primitive genera. Most commonly rhizomes are clothed with scales, and the variety is wide: they may be yellow or orange to brown and black; narrow or broad; flimsy and thin-walled or stout and thick-walled; spreading or close-fitting (these are called appressed); smooth-margined or toothed.

Some scales are so striking that the plant takes its common name from them. The squirrel's-foot, hare's-foot, bear's-foot, and so on are so named because their epiphytic creeping rhizomes are covered with white or golden scales that give them the appearance of animal feet. But a word of caution: never get into an argument as to whether a plant you're trying to identify is a deer's-foot or a rabbit's-foot. There are dozens of these types around, and the names are often interchangeable and used indiscriminately. You and your opponent may both be right.

A beginner who wants to start educating himself about scales would do well to start with the spleenworts and the shoestring ferns, whose rhizomes are covered with a distinctive type of scale called the clathrate scale. The cells of these scales have a combination of thick black vertical walls and thin, iridescent horizontal walls, resulting in a shimmer of color that makes them look like leaded stained-glass windows. They can be easily recognized with a little practice, and the amateur can go on with confidence to more difficult problems.

Some plants can be recognized by the fact that they display combinations of hairs and scales, or structures transi-

43

tional between hairs and scales. *Anemia* has only hairs, but its close relative *Mohria* has broad scales on the rhizome and the lower part of the leaf. The scales gradually become narrower toward the top of the frond, until at the top they are no longer scales but one-cell-wide hairs, the same as appear on *Anemia*.

Among other genera that can be identified by their hairs is *Thelypteris*. It is particularly helpful to learn to recognize the needlelike hairs of this large family, since *Thelypteris* species are often weeds, and if you are experimenting with baby ferns in a greenhouse it makes little sense to spend time nursing a weed along to maturity when the same effort might be spent on a fern more worth cultivating.

Glandular hairs—one to several cells long with glandular tips—can also act as markers. In the eastern United States

The lower surface of the silverback fern (*Pityrogramma calomelanos*) is covered with tiny white wax glands.

a common species with abundant aromatic glandular hairs is the hay-scented fern (*Dennstaedtia punctilobula*). Elsewhere there are ferns whose short glandular hairs produce globules of white or yellow wax. The undersides of the leaves of *Pityrogramma*, *Notholaena*, *Cheilanthes*, and others are so closely covered with these glands that when ruffled by air the fronds look white or yellow. Not surprisingly, the common names for them are silverback and goldback.

There are also hairs that grow one cell wide at the tip but more than one cell thick at the base. The thin hair-tip tends to fall off, leaving the stout base, which is protrusive and substantial enough to be called a spine. Many species of *Hypolepis* produce these spines, and a group of them constitute a real bramble patch, something to stay out of. The

The leaf stalks of tree ferns often bear stout spines.

spines on the leaf bases of tree ferns are particularly wicked. On the Mexican tree fern *Nephelea mexicana* they grow heavy, black, and curved like weapons. An adventure with spine-bearing ferns can leave both your clothing and your skin in a nasty mess.

An odd, somewhat atypical collection of hairs is sometimes found mixed in with the sporangia in a sorus. These are occasionally the same kinds of hairs found on the leaf blade itself, but more often they are distinct; they are called paraphyses (pa-*raf*-i-sees). There is no clear definition of their functions or even of how they originate. Some, which we take to be aborted sporangia, we call sporangiasters. Others are club-shaped, with long cells at the base and several short, broad cells near the tip. While some paraphyses show up mixed among the sporangia, others are found on the sporangia—in some cases looking like small glands on the stalk of a sporangium, in others like horns on the sporangium. These are usually distinctive for individual species or genera, and therefore useful in classification.

Color. Not only do ferns surprise us with unfernlike shapes—sometimes they're not even green. Most striking are the juvenile leaves of the maidenhairs and of *Blechnum*, *Doodia*, and *Woodwardia*. Their crosiers and freshly expanded leaves start out in varying shades of pink before they mature into the more traditional green. The unrolling leaves of *Didymochlaena* are the color of bronze. And of course there are the silverbacks and goldbacks, with the wax glands we have already described creating their pleasant color.

There is no such thing, either, as a standard fern green; the green fronds come in varying shades. Some of the ferns from arid climates, such as *Pellaea* and *Cheilanthes*, are

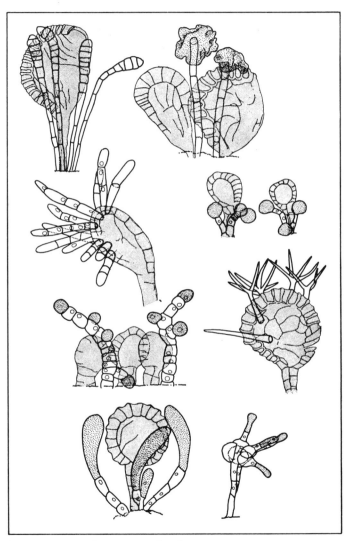

Paraphyses, special structures within the
sori, may be hairlike, club-shaped,
or glandular. They may be among the sporangia
or on the sporangia themselves.

47

gray-green. The bird's-nest is yellow-green, and Ben Franklin's *Dryopteris intermedia*—the evergreen wood fern—is frequently bluish-green. *Anemia makrinii's* fronds, also blue-green in color, have a metallic sheen as well.

A number of variegated forms are popular in cultivation. *Pteris quadriaurita* var. *argyraea, P. cretica* cv. *Albolineata,* and *P. ensiformis* var. *victoriae* have a broad white band down the center of each pinna or segment. The Japanese painted fern, *Athyrium niponicum* cv. *Pictum (A. goeringianum* cv. *Pictum)*, is a veritable peacock, combining green, gray, and burgundy red in its fronds. Several species of *Athyrium* show red in the leaf stalks, but *A. niponicum* makes the most flamboyant display.

sori

The fruiting dots, or sori, on the undersurface of the fern leaf take many forms, but generally they are consistent for each genus or group of genera. You will usually see them as round dots or as a continuous line along the leaf margin, though in some species they will be elongated along the midvein or another vein. Most of the time they are protected by a special flap, the indusium, which covers the sorus when it is young. As the sporangia mature and get ready to release the spores, the indusium bends back or withers.

In the case of *Hemionitis* there is no indusium, and the soral arrangement thus revealed is very interesting. The sporangia are found along all the veins, following their entire netted pattern. The sori follow the veins also in *Pityrogramma*, but these veins are not netted and are hidden by the waxy covering, so that the sporangia appear like specks of pepper in the white or yellow wax.

In some of the more primitive fern groups the sporangia

48

The indusia covering the sori of the
southern wood fern (*Dryopteris ludoviciana*)
lift up to expose the mature sporangia.

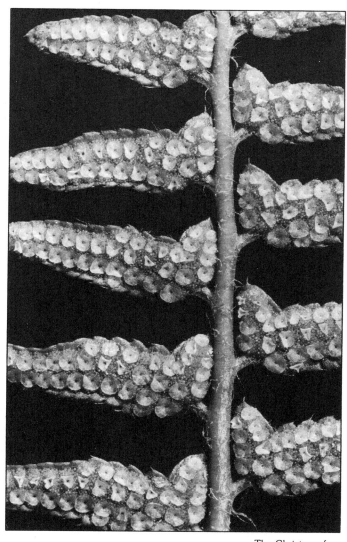

50

The Christmas fern
(*Polystichum acrostichoides*) has large sori
covered with round indusia.

The sori of the silvery spleenwort
(*Athyrium thelypterioides*) are elongate along
the veins and covered by indusia.

52

The bracken has its sori along the frond margins, which fold over to protect the sporangia in their young stages.

are not organized into clearly distinct sori. Rather, they develop individually or collect into large formless masses, as in the royal and cinnamon ferns of the genus *Osmunda*.

dimorphism

In most kinds of ferns all the leaves look alike, and all perform two functions: they manufacture food through photosynthesis and they produce spores. In some groups, however, there is a dramatic difference between fertile and sterile leaves. Fertile leaves, or fertile parts of leaves, may be completely devoid of leafy tissue. They consist of barely more than the veins and the sporangia. At maturity, their color is brown or golden, so that they can be clearly distinguished from the sterile or vegetative leaves, which are green. This phenomenon—two different forms on the same plant—is called dimorphism, and generally all the members of a given genus show it. Thus, such groups as *Osmunda* and *Polybotrya* have distinctive fertile fronds, but *Osmunda* has developed further complexities. In the cinnamon fern (*O. cinnamomea*) the leaves are either entirely fertile or entirely sterile, the fertile ones coming up ahead of the others in the spring, dropping their spores in early summer, then withering away. The interrupted fern (*O. claytoniana*) has only a few pairs of sporangia-bearing, fertile pinnae in the middle of each frond. The royal fern (*O. regalis*) is fertile only at the tip third of the frond; this is the peculiarity that gives it the colloquial name "flowering fern."

Other combinations and variations abound. The adder's-tongue and the rattlesnake fern (*Botrychium*) bear their sporangia on an erect fertile spike arising from the leaf stalk. The genus *Anemia* is highly distinctive: its sporangia are limited to the base pair of pinnae, which have lost nearly all

53

their leaf tissue and evolved an erect habit. *Anemia* thus appears to be marching through life holding two golden candles high in the air. The ostrich fern and its close relative the sensitive fern (*Onoclea sensibilis*) have distinct brown fertile fronds, but these fertile fronds are not tender as they are in most dimorphic-fronded species, and do not wither away. They are tough and woody, their segments inrolled like bunches of grapes. After the vegetative leaves have died down for the winter, these fertile segments remain standing at attention. In late winter they open to release their spores, sometimes on snow.

fern allies

In that remote time when the first plants appeared, some developed large, complex leaves and others did not. The leafy ones came to be called ferns; the others, which have simple needlelike or scalelike leaves, each with a single unbranched vein, are the plants we call fern allies. Like the ferns, they reproduce by spores. They also have the same sort of life history: spore reproduction is followed by a free-living gametophyte generation. Consequently, they are grouped with the ferns as lower vascular plants, or pteridophytes. Nevertheless, the term "fern allies" is a misnomer, for research has now shown us that these plants are not at all closely allied to the ferns, nor, for that matter, to each other.

We have remnants of these groups today in our whisk ferns, clubmosses, spikemosses, quillworts, and horsetails. Even visually they are rarely mistaken for ferns. Some look like mosses, others like flowering plants. With few exceptions, present-day horsetails and clubmosses grow at most a few feet tall. It is strange to realize that in the forests of

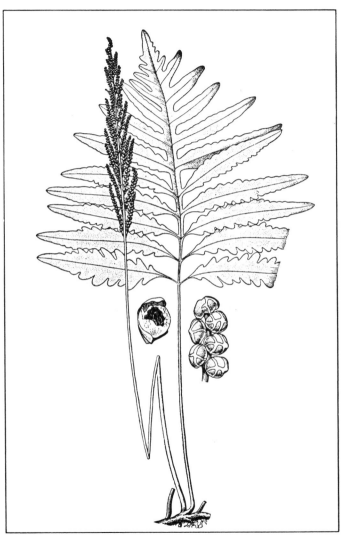

The sensitive fern has two kinds of
fronds—vegetative (food-producing) fronds and
specialized spine-bearing fronds.

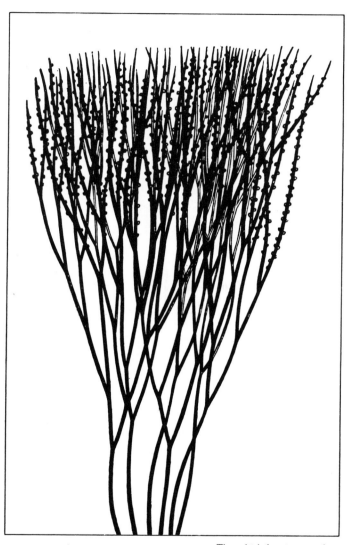

56

The whisk fern is not a fern
at all. It bears no roots or leaves but
consists of green, forking stems.

250 million years ago they soared gigantically, 100 feet and more, with trunks 3 feet in diameter. The ancient ferns have been mistakenly credited with this gigantism, which in actuality only their allies achieved. Ferns were certainly abundant and made up much of the earth's vegetation (there were also some early conifers), but contrary to popular belief relatively few of the ferns were overwhelmingly tall trees.

Whisk ferns *(Psilotum).* These are without doubt the simplest vascular plants we know of today. They have no roots or leaves, and consist of an underground rhizome that sends up erect aerial branches that fork repeatedly, making them look more like a bundle of green sticks than anything else. On the stems are tiny scalelike protuberances without veins, and large three-lobed sporangia. For a long time botanists believed the whisks to be modern representatives of

The running pine bears erect cones and is one of the most widespread clubmosses in the temperate regions of the world.

a primitive group of vascular plants known from fossils 400 million years old, but no signs of the whisk ferns or their relatives have been discovered from the intervening period. Their anatomy and chemical components definitely place them outside the fern camp. They stand alone; we just do not know what their origin is.

There are only two species known. The more widespread, *P. nudum*, occurs in many tropical areas, growing on tree trunks or among rocks. Some atypical forms grow wild in Japan, and during the early nineteenth century they became almost a·cult object there, the subject of many books and of enthusiastic cultivation that still persists today. They grow well in a greenhouse and may also appear spontaneously, especially around the bases of palm trees.

Tmesipteris (meh-*sip*-ter-is) is a relative of *Psilotum* found in the South Pacific. It also lacks roots, but does have small, single-veined leaves. It is rarely cultivated.

Clubmosses *(Lycopodium)*.   These have creeping stems

The running cedar sends up short treelike stalks with flattened branches from its long-creeping rhizome.

and aerial branches with needlelike leaves arranged in spirals. The most widespread is probably the running pine (*L. clavatum*), which creeps along the ground branching profusely, looking like a coarse moss. Slender stalks arise at the tips of some branches, bearing club-shaped cones.

Clubmosses like the running cedar (*L. flabelliforme*) have long, creeping, underground stems and flattened aerial branches with tiny scalelike leaves. Their cones are borne four to a branch, like candelabra. These are the plants that pull up like evergreen ropes, and they have been so carelessly plundered to make Christmas wreaths that they are now widely protected by law.

In more tropical regions there is the nodding clubmoss (*L. cernuum*), which grows 2 or 3 feet high and displays a

The nodding clubmoss
may stand as tall as 3 feet and is
abundant in tropical regions.

small nodding cone at the tip of each of its many branches. Other tropical species are epiphytic, hanging down from tree trunks in wet, undisturbed forests. The branches of *L. phlegmaria* hang down 2 to 3 feet, with tassellike cones at the tips.

While most clubmosses bear their sporangia in cones, the fir clubmoss and shining clubmoss (*L. selago* and *L. lucidulum*) secrete their sporangia in the axils of normal vegetative leaves. These plants also have a backup means of reproduction: among their leaves are specialized buds called gemmae, which fall off and develop into new plants.

The tassel clubmoss (*Lycopodium phlegmaria*) hangs from trees with tassellike cones at the branch tips.

Clubmoss spores sometimes take years to germinate. The spore coats are so tough that they must be softened with strong acid before there's much chance that they will germinate in cultivation. Also, the prothalli develop underground and are difficult to find.

Many other temperate clubmosses cannot be cultivated because of their need for certain fungi (*mycorrhizae*) that grow in their native soil. However, the fir clubmoss and the shining clubmoss are exceptions that can be grown successfully. A determined gardener might also do well with several of the epiphytic varieties by using osmunda fiber

Lycopodium squarrosum also hangs from tree trunks, but it bears its sporangia among the leaves rather than in cones.

or sphagnum moss instead of soil, and providing high humidity.

Spikemosses *(Selaginella)*. The spikemosses are like miniature clubmosses, with the same scalelike, spirally arranged leaves. They bear their spores in somewhat unusual cones, which in cross section show up generally as square rather than round. They produce not one kind of spore, but two: large females (megaspores) and small males (microspores), growing in separate sporangia. The microsporangia are oval and smooth, each containing several hundred dustlike spores. The female containers, the megasporangia, are lobed and hold only four spores, which are so large that they frequently can be seen with the naked eye. *Selaginella exaltata*, a large tropical spikemoss, produces spores as large as 1,500 microns—nearly a sixteenth of an inch—in diam-

Spikemosses such as *Selaginella pallescens* are common terrestrial plants, especially in tropical regions. They bear their sporangia in spikelike cones at the branch tips.

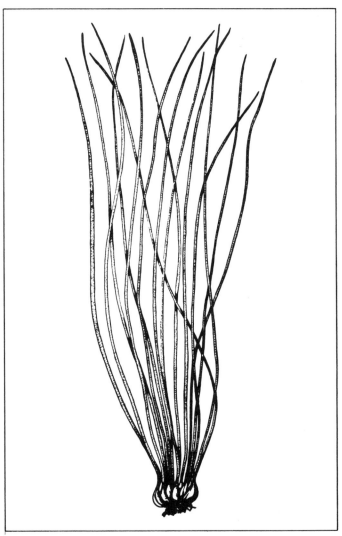

Quillworts have grasslike leaves
and grow mostly underwater. The sporangia are
located in the swollen leaf bases.

eter. I have seen these white giants of the spore world bounce and roll on the floor like small tapioca balls.

There are two distinct groups of spikemosses. One, common to the dry areas of the western United States and Mexico, looks like moss, with tiny needlelike leaves spaced all around the stem. It is usually found in tufts on rocks or on the ground. Most of the six hundred known spikemosses belong to the second group, those that prefer wet areas. Some of these are creepers, but some are suberect or even treelike, growing perhaps a few feet tall. Their recognizable leaves are arranged on the stems in four rows: two lateral rows of moderately large leaves, and on the top side of the stem two rows of smaller and differently shaped leaves.

The spikemosses of this second group—called heterophyllous, since they bear differing leaves—are quite easy to grow. The creeping species make good ground cover in a greenhouse, and can be equally useful in terrariums or bottle gardens, where they can get the high humidity that is absolutely essential. *Selaginella kraussiana* is the most widespread species in cultivation, with two attractive varieties to offer: var. *aurea*, with bright yellowish leaves, and var. *braunii*, which has a bushy habit somewhat more erect than the usual creeping style of most spikemosses. You might also investigate *S. willdenovii* and *S. uncinata*, which are vinelike with metallic blue-green leaves.

Quillworts *(Isoetes)*. These are plants you will rarely see. They grow in many parts of the world, but they grow underwater or in swampy areas, and they resemble grass more than they do any of the lower vascular plants. Each quillwort consists of a cormlike stem from which arises some fleshy roots and many grasslike leaves. The leaves are linear; they have a single vein and contain air spaces separated by ribs that can be seen externally. The sporangia are embedded in the leaf bases, hard to find. Like the spike-mosses, quillworts have two kinds of spores. The mega-spores are not as large as those of the spikemosses, but like them, they bear sharply distinctive ornamentation, which is valuable for identification.

These somewhat eerie plants are definitely of ancient origin. They are actually reduced versions of ancestors that were among the largest trees of the Carboniferous period. They sometimes proliferate and cover acres of pond bot-tom, and since quillwort species have a peculiar tendency to vary slightly from pond to pond, scientists often cannot tell exactly which species they have picked up. There is not enough differentiation among the variants to establish a new species, yet not enough resemblance for the botanist to be certain which of the approximately sixty recognized species he has. Nobody has yet figured out an explanation for this odd characteristic, which keeps us from being sure just how many species there actually are.

Quillworts are fairly promising for the home gardener. They can be grown in a greenhouse in a pot set in a dish of water, or submerged in an aquarium.

Horsetails and scouring rushes *(Equisetum).*
Horsetails also can be traced back to the Carboniferous period. They have some easily recognizable characteristics: their aerial stems are jointed and pull apart easily, giving them the nickname "puzzlegrass," and the leaves that grow at these joints are produced in whorls. The leaves, which look like small black or white teeth, make no contribution to the plant's food manufacturing. Food production goes on in the hollow green stems, which are ridged on the surface. Because the plant deposits silica in its cell walls, these ridges

65

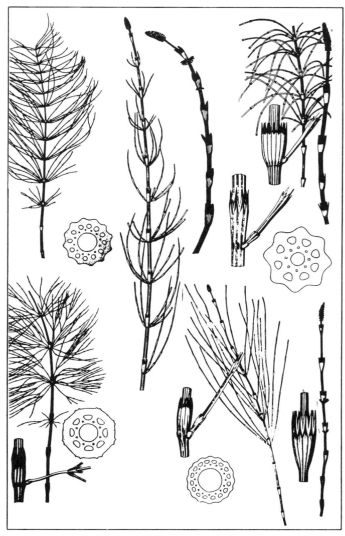

66

Horsetails and scouring rushes have
hollow green grooved stems with only minute
scalelike leaves at the joints.

become so coarse that you can use them to file your fingernails. They were the "scouring rushes" American colonists used for cleaning pots and trenchers, and even today they are used to file clarinet reeds.

The spores are formed in spore cases inside cones at the stem tips. In the common horsetail (*E. arvense*) the cones grow on special ephemeral stems that die down right after the spores are shed. The spores themselves, being green, have a more rapid metabolism and so are relatively short-lived. If they do not get out and germinate within two days, they lose their chance. To this end they are round and smooth and bear four long strings, or elaters, which, coiling and straightening in response to changes in humidity, help them to detach swiftly from the sporangia.

When horsetails do take, they form great stands and are difficult to eradicate. Generally this kind of expansion is the result of vegetative, rather than spore, reproduction. The wide-creeping underground stems send up new growth over wide areas; also, fragments of the plants fall or break off and root, initiating further proliferation.

Although most of the fifteen species of *Equisetum* are under 3 feet tall, there are three giants in tropical America that grow to 20 feet high and more. To wander among them is a kind of science-fiction experience. I well remember the first time I encountered a stand of the giant horsetail in Mexico. I had the feeling that I had found my way backward into a Carboniferous forest, and half expected dinosaurs to appear among the horsetails.

**reproduction,
nature's way**

Spores are no longer the "magic dust" of times gone by, but they still fascinate us. We are intrigued that this insignificant-looking matter conceals the secret of life. So perhaps, in the interests of truth, I should point out that while ferns do propagate by spores, they have also evolved a backup method to ensure ongoing life. This is vegetative reproduction, which we look at in Chapter 5.

As a matter of fact, most ferns in the wild are produced vegetatively, which means that they result from a bud formed on a parent plant, or from a piece that breaks off an older plant and finds rooting space. Nonetheless, spores are there, and they do work. Examining them is not only botanically interesting, but will give you a background if you want to try growing your own plants from spores—an altogether feasible project.

how spores work

The spore cases (sporangia) in which the spores of a mature plant are borne are found almost always on the undersides of the leaves, in clusters (sori) that vary from a few sporangia to about a hundred. In a developing sporangium the central cell divides to form two cells, each of which goes on to divide so that four are formed, and the process continues until there are sixteen cells in place of the original one. Finally, each of these sixteen "spore mother cells" divides by a special two-step process called meiosis to form four spores, thus making a total of sixty-four spores in a sporangium.

This is the process as it operates in most modern ferns.

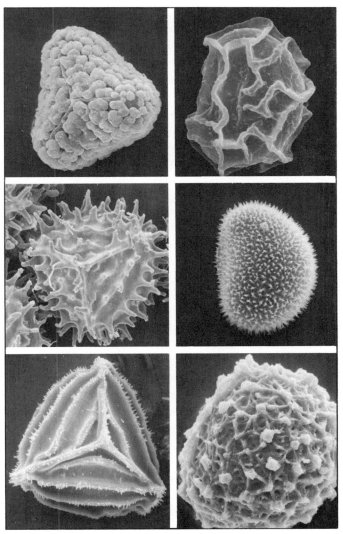

Fern spores are extremely diverse.
These photographs, taken with a scanning
electron microscope, show a few of
the many types found.

More primitive, less highly evolved ferns produce as many as 128, 256, 512, or even more spores in each sporangium, a throwback to the primeval condition when thousands were produced. Even now, the sporangia of the fern allies and some primitive ferns usually contain thousands of spores.

Basically there are two spore shapes: bean-shaped with a single line of scar marking the place where the spore broke away from its three sibling spores, and tetrahedral with a Y-shaped breakaway scar. However, as the four spores break apart and become distinct from one another, each develops an outer ornamentation that individualizes it. Sometimes these decorations—spines, bumps, ridges, pitting, a raised network, high wavy crests—are minor, but in some families they are marked and different for each species, making them especially useful in identification and in establishing relationships among species.

The markings can also have geological importance. The outer layer of the spore wall is composed of a complex substance called sporopollenin, which is extremely resistant to decomposition. In rock deposits many millions of years old, spores have been found with their walls intact and nearly unchanged. Sometimes the rock can be dissolved with acids, leaving the spores exposed and easy to study. Since we have a pretty good knowledge of the spore markings of modern ferns, we can establish relationships and determine which kinds of plants lived many millions of years ago. This method also works with higher, pollen-producing plants, whose pollen grains are the rough equivalent of fern spores. Knowing the kinds of plants associated with particular climates, we can learn a lot from pollen and spore deposits about climatic changes in the past. Some distinctive

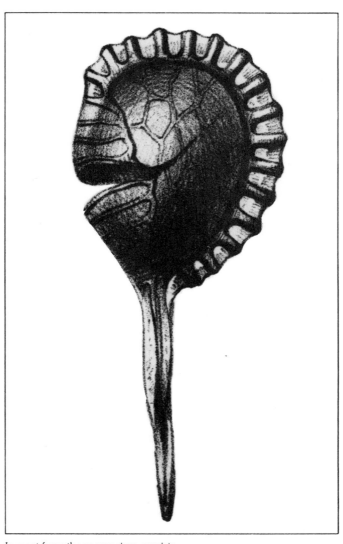

In most ferns the sporangium consists
of a stalk and a capsule that contains
the spores. The capsule opens by means of the
contraction of the thick-walled
row of cells known as the annulus.

73

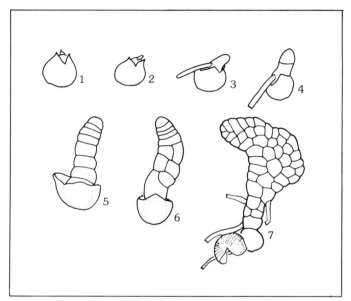

fern spores are correlated with petroleum deposits, so their study is especially useful.

Separated, decorated with their final distinctive markings, the spores are mature, and the sporangium opens to release them. This opening is not a random splitting. It occurs at a special place on the spore case. A band of thick-walled cells, called the annulus, contracts to create the opening. The opening itself is slow, but then the spores are abruptly catapulted outward into the environment. Some fall to the ground fairly soon. Others are carried by air drafts for varying distances—several feet, several miles—before falling to earth.

With sixty-four spores per sporangium, perhaps fifty sporangia per sorus, hundreds of sori per leaf, and several

Spore germination. The spore cracks open (1) and the contained cell emerges and puts out a hairlike rhizoid (2, 3, 4). Divisions make a filament (5) that later broadens to form the prothallus (6, 7).

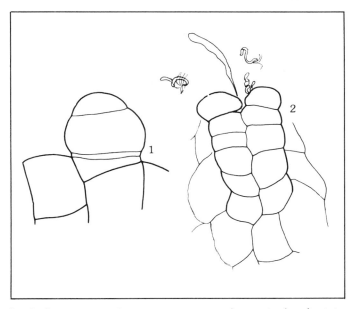

fertile leaves per plant, it is common for a single plant to produce millions of spores in one season. So the world should be covered with ferns. But it is not. The sad truth is that most spores don't make it. To germinate, they must fall on shaded, moist places where there is not already such vigorous vegetation that they will be crowded out. A muddy shaded bank with a constant supply of moisture is ideal. Most spores, however, fall on less suitable spots and die before they have a chance to germinate. Others may germinate, but soon go under for lack of moisture.

The fortunate spore that comes to rest on a hospitable spot germinates as it absorbs water and then splits open along the scar line, the single cell within becoming larger and longer. It turns green, establishing the presence of chlo-

The antheridium (1) releases
the sperms, which swim to the archegonium (2)
and down its neck to fertilize the egg.

rophyll, which enables it to manufacture its own food through photosynthesis. Its chief need is for water, and to search for this it sends out a hairlike rhizoid that acts like a root, absorbing minerals along with essential water from the soil. The green cell, continuing its elongation, divides; there are now two cells. Soon, with more divisions, a filament has been formed, and more rhizoids are sent down. As growth proceeds, some of the cells near the filament tip divide laterally so that it is broadened. The structure, which is now a plantlet, or prothallus, continues to push both forward and laterally to form a heart-shaped pad of green tissue, its base clothed with many rhizoids.

The entire prothallus is usually only a quarter-inch across. Its midrib is a few cells thick, but it is only a single cell thick on its "wings." Yet it is on the lower surface of these seemingly fragile prothalli that the sexual part of the plant's life history gets under way. On the wings and among the rhizoids are the antheridia, tiny beadlike structures that produce sperm. When a surface film of water is present, the antheridial protective lid is released and several sperms emerge. Spiral-shaped and equipped with numerous long flagellae that enable it to move, each sperm swims rapidly toward the "female" components, the archegonia—several tiny, chimney-shaped projections that occur along the thickened midrib of the prothallus. In the base of each archegonium is a single egg cell; when this is mature and ready for fertilization, the tip of the chimney opens to release the fluid contents of the neck. This effluent attracts the swimming sperms, which follow it down the neck canal; one sperm then fertilizes the waiting egg.

The sex cells are called gametes; thus the prothallus is often described as the gametophyte generation in the plant's life cycle. The parent plant that has produced the spores is the sporophyte.

The fertilized egg, embedded in the prothallus, grows and divides to form a multicellular structure, and embarks on the familiar process of cell specialization. Part of the new growth differentiates as a root, part becomes the first leaf, part protrudes as an infant stem that will grow out to produce new roots and leaves. A young fern has now been established, and the prothallus, having completed its job, withers away.

If a growing fern is kept under observation, it is possible to see that each new leaf is a little larger and often more dissected than the preceding one. However, it takes some time for truly mature leaves to appear. It may be months, or even years, before the plant is strong enough to produce fertile, sporangia-bearing leaves that will go on to play their part in the continuing cycle.

The time a fern takes to complete its life cycle from spore to spore-producing plant depends on the group it belongs to. Some ferns require two years for the whole process. But some species of *Thelypteris* take only six months, and the water fern *Ceratopteris* completes its cycle in only three months. In some ways, speed means success: it reflects the plant's ability to compete in its world, its aggressiveness in taking over bare soil and filling up spaces available for germination. The percentage of spores that survive and germinate is also a key factor. Together with the vigor of the prothalli, it helps dictate which species become the tough weeds of the fern world and which the more fragile rarities. No matter how vigorous a prothallus may be, it is small and inconspicuous, so well concealed from the naked eye that finding one in the wild, or even in a greenhouse, is a real challenge. In the wild, you might try looking for prothalli near ferns, especially on muddy banks or on the mud in swampy areas. But if you want to satisfy your curiosity the easy way, look in a humid greenhouse where ferns are already being cultivated. It should be relatively easy to discover prothalli and even young ferns growing on the sides of moist pots, or on undisturbed surfaces of soil—the equivalent of nature's muddy banks.

Since our best current knowledge appears to downplay the importance of spores in fern reproduction, you might want to add to your own—and perhaps the general—information by investigating which ferns in your area do reproduce by spores, and to what extent. Are all species reproducing? Where are the gametophytes in relation to the parent plants? How rapidly do they develop from spore to mature plant? How far do they develop before winter: to prothallus, to young sporophyte? Are all spores shed before summer ends? Recent studies show that some ferns retain a portion of their spores within the sporangia longer than was previously believed—for several months, well into the winter and the following spring—and that these spores remain viable. Is this one of nature's cautious backup plans, to ensure against a large percentage of failure in the spores shed during the summer?

Heterospory. In a few of the water ferns (*Marsilea, Salvinia, Azolla,* and relatives) and fern allies (*Selaginella* and *Isoetes*) two kinds of spores are produced, large female spores (megaspores) and small male spores (microspores). Each type forms in different sporangia. The megaspores germinate by cracking open, exposing a few archegonia. When this happens, the microspores release a few sperms, which swim to the archegonia and find an egg to fertilize.

The condition of having two kinds of spores is called heterospory, and is a step toward the evolution of the seed way of life. The microspores function like the pollen grains of seed plants. However, in the seed plant the fertilized egg develops into an embryo and then rests, protected by special layers called integuments. This, of course, is the seed, a stage that the ferns do not have.

Apogamy. Although most ferns pass through the above steps, occasionally there are irregularities in a plant's makeup that direct it to follow a slightly different route. In one variation, sex is by-passed entirely. Spores germinate to form the prothalli, and the sex organs (antheridia and archegonia) may also form, but they do not function. Instead the prothallus develops a bud, usually a slight swelling on the underside of the notch of the heart-shaped prothallus, surrounded by hairs. As it continues to enlarge, the bud produces a leaf. This represents a distinct departure from the scenario of normal fertilization, in which the root is always produced first, before any other part of the plant. In fact, several leaves may form before the first root makes its appearance. Once the plant is established, the prothallus withers and vanishes. Since there is no fusion of gametes (sperm and egg) the process is called apogamy ("without gametes").

Apogamy occurs in more fern groups, and with more frequency, than is generally realized. Some commonly cultivated plants like the Japanese holly fern and the Cretan brake follow an apogamous life style. It has its advantages, particularly in situations where fertilization would be impeded by lack of water, which is necessary to help convey the sperm to the egg. Since apogamous plants circumvent the whole fertilization process, they can often produce new

79

80

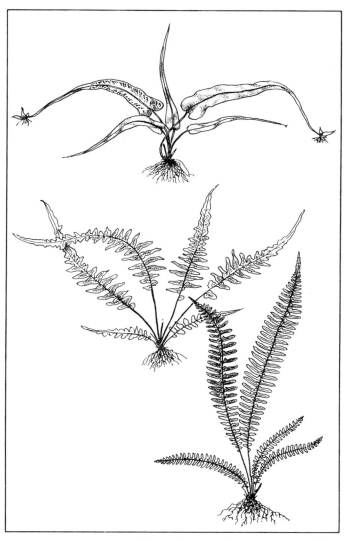

The walking fern (*Camptosorus rhizophyllus,* top) and the ebony spleenwort (*Asplenium platyneuron,* bottom) occasionally hybridize to form Scott's spleenwort (*Asplenosorus ebenoides*).

plants more rapidly and successfully than can ferns that rely on sexual reproduction.

Apospory. Another alternate life style is apospory, reproduction without spores. The sporophyte plant produces gametophytes directly on the frond, without having first produced spores. This is very rare, and likely to occur only under special circumstances. However, in Trinidad, Tobago, and Grenada there are two species of *Trichomanes* that regularly produce small gametophytes on their fronds. They do this by means of tiny chains of cells that are borne on toothlike projections along the frond margins. When ready, each chain falls from the leaf and forms a gametophyte. In their turn, the gametophytes in these plants will go on to produce sporophytes apogamously.

hybridization

Quite frequently ferns hybridize, all on their own. The sperm from one prothallus finds its way to a mature egg on the prothallus of another plant and fertilizes it. It works only when the two prothalli are related—members either of the same genus or of closely connected genera.

Hybridization does not often produce a new species, because hybrid ferns are usually sterile. The spores abort, appearing as crumpled blobs of spore-wall material. The hybrid plant continues to grow, and may reproduce vegetatively, but spore reproduction is denied it.

Occasionally, through a happy genetic accident involving the chromosome make-up of the spores, the union does create a fertile hybrid. This is indeed a new species, since it is different from all others and can reproduce by spores.

In some genera—notably *Dryopteris*, *Asplenium*, and *Diplazium*—the species mix quite promiscuously with oth-

81

ers, forming great hybrid complexes. It's interesting to know that the new plants are out there somewhere, but the knowledge is not of much use to most amateurs because hybrids are generally so intermediate between the parent plants that they are not distinct enough to the eye to be singled out. Microscopic examination of spores and chromosomes is often the only sure way to identify them.

This lack of distinctiveness naturally doesn't stop horticulturists and research botanists from creating hybrids in the laboratory for their own purposes. They do it in several ways. In the simplest, the spores of two distinct species are sown together and the experimenter sits back and hopes that crossing will occur. Results are more predictable when a female gametophyte is placed next to a male gametophyte of another species. Sometimes a male gametophyte is placed in a drop of water to encourage the discharge of sperm; then a female gametophyte of another species is put into the water for an hour or two, and planted. To eliminate the possibility of self-fertilization, an experimenter may carefully cut off the part of a gametophyte with the archegonia (around the notch) and place it next to the basal, antheridial portion of a gametophyte of another species. The amateur who could do this successfully, though, would probably have to be a skilled surgeon whose hobby just happens to be botany.

Generally speaking, hybridization can be an interesting diversion for a fern fancier who is not expecting to set the plant world on fire. He may—as nature herself does—come up with a variation whose leaf dissection is intermediate between that of the two plants he has crossed, and if he's not looking for much more, it's certainly worth trying.

Even in the hands of commercial fern growers, hybridization is not a practical means of producing new fern varieties. The numbers of our flowering plants have of course been enormously increased in this way, but crossing ferns is not as rewarding. It is tedious and unreliable work, and the number of truly new plants that result has been very small.

How then do we get our infrequent new varieties? We wait for nature to hand them out. We get them from random mutations, spontaneously created without man's interference, the occasional oddballs in the mass of "normal" sporelings.

**growing your own:
from spores**

modern research has thrown some cold water on the idea that spores are all-important in the natural propagation of ferns. But under cultivation the story is quite different. Growing new plants from spores collected from your own ferns is simple, rewarding, even exciting. Once you understand the growth process, spores are easy to collect and store. They can be sent through the mail: you can exchange them by letter with friends anywhere in the world. The return in numbers of plants is gratifying. Best of all, it takes no special equipment, just information, patience, and care.

collecting the spores

Timing is everything. Like the old wives' herbs that had to be cut precisely at midnight on Midsummer's Eve, spores must be collected at just the right stage of ripeness, because for your purposes the only usable spore is a ripe one. If it is too young, it will not germinate. If you wait too long, it won't be there at all—the sporangium will have opened and released it, and it will be taking its chances at nature's hands. So the first step in spore propagation is to become familiar with the appearance of the sporangia in all their phases— immature, ripe, and spent.

What you are looking for is dark color. Most spores are dark brown or black at maturity, and the ripe sori show this color. It's therefore fairly easy to avoid collecting immature spores, because unripe sori are very pale, whitish or faintly

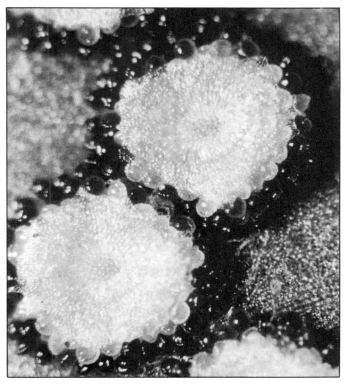

green, and barely noticeable. At the other end of the process—when the spores have burst forth and winged off—there is also a characteristic color to clue you to the fact that you've missed the boat. After the sporangia have opened and released the spores, they display a tannish color, and consequently the sori in which they are grouped appear tan.

But there are a few pitfalls that only experience and sharp observation can teach you to avoid. Some genera, like *Polypodium*, have golden spores. The sori are therefore

Close-up of two sori. The white indusia protect the sporangia, which appear around their margins. The mature sporangia here are black; a few lighter-colored immature sporangia can also be seen.

golden, and it is not always easy to distinguish the mature golden sori from old tan sori. Also, maturation in any plant is not uniform. Sporangia mature first at the bottom of the frond. This means that on a single frond the sporangia at the bottom may be empty, having released their ripe spores; at the tip end the spores may be too young; but in the middle they may be just right for collection. Further, even within a single sorus the sporangia do not all mature at once. There is almost always a mixture of the mature and the juvenile. A fairly good magnifying glass—a 10-power hand lens is adequate—is essential when you are trying to identify the different stages of sorus development.

When you have spotted the fronds (or pinnae or segments) that bear ripe spores, pick them and place them face-down on white paper to dry. Smooth paper is best, so that the spores can be easily tapped off when ready. Cover them with a second sheet and add a light weight to keep the spores from blowing away. The ripe spores will start dropping to the paper immediately, and after a day your bits of fern will have shed about all they are going to. Remove the protective covering, then carefully lift the leaf and give it a final, very gentle tap to give any undecided spores a last chance to detach themselves. You want them if they're ready, but you don't want to tap so hard that you knock onto your paper sporangia, which will dilute your product.

You now have pure spores, ready to go to work for the survival of their species. Store them in glassine envelopes, paper envelopes, sterilized vials, or gelatin capsules. Capsules can be obtained from your friendly pharmacist, especially when he knows what you want them for.

An alternate method is to pick off a fertile bit of leaf, check with your lens to make sure it still has spores, and store it directly in an envelope. If your working sample is a piece of frond with no loose spores, you can make it usable by scraping off its sori onto a sheet of paper. Tap the paper gently until the material on it shifts toward the edge. The spores, you will discover, remain in place longer than the chaff and old sporangia, which slide quickly to the edge and can be discarded. It is important to get rid of the sporangia, because they harbor fungus spores, and you don't want to risk contaminating your pure spore culture with these.

Still another way to separate the spores from the sporangia is to put the sorus material through a sieve. Make your own by folding two or three layers of nylon stocking over the mouth of a container. When you press the scraped-off sorus material through this, the spores will go through, and most of the unwanted sporangia will remain behind.

No matter how you package your spores, keep them cool and dry. Heat reduces their viability. Your refrigerator is probably the best place to store them until you are ready to use them.

I have germinated spores of the purple cliff-brake that were nearly fifty years old. I have also heard of spores that germinated after a hundred years, but this report has never been documented. Most fern spores will remain viable for several months, and some for several years. With the passage of time, though, viability decreases and fewer spores will germinate. In part, their durability depends on how they are dried. When spores are exposed to heat, their viability is reduced and may even be destroyed completely. ·

Spores that show green color, indicating chlorophyll within, are generally short-lived. The ostrich fern and the sensitive fern appear to be exceptions; both have green spores, but these remain alive for a year or more without special treatment. The green-tinged spores of horsetails and filmy ferns, however, die in a few days. Dr. Richard Hauke, an authority on the horsetails, has traveled to Central America and India to germinate horsetail spores on the spot; those sent by air mail were always dead on arrival.

how to sow

Containers. Use clear plastic or glass containers with clear, tight-fitting lids. No air must be allowed to enter, since it dries out the culture and brings in foreign spores. Jelly jars, freezer cartons, even plastic drinking cups tightly covered with plastic film will serve well. If you use a glass dish, smear a bit of Vaseline around the rim to help create an airtight seal when the top goes on.

One of the best setups for sowing in quantity is made by placing 2¼-inch-square plastic flowerpots in an ordinary plastic shoebox, available at any dime store; eighteen of them will just fit. The shoebox cover keeps the humidity up for all eighteen pots.

Sowing medium. For most fern species, you can use any one of several sowing media: soil mix, sphagnum, plain water (see page 97), broken flowerpots, osmunda fiber. My favorite is pure sphagnum, either milled or long-strand. Some people swear by a mixture of sphagnum and sand. Others prefer a mixture of equal parts of leaf mold, soil, and sand; peat or vermiculite can be substituted for the leaf mold. You can also use presterilized packaged African violet mix.

Warning: any mixture containing leaf mold or soil must be sterilized. Spores of fungi, mosses, and algae, as well as countless little animals, are out there waiting to eat or overwhelm the young gametophytes, and your protégés have to be protected from them. Pure sphagnum doesn't need to be sterilized, since it is too acid to harbor many contaminants, but it doesn't hurt to be on the safe side by dousing it with boiling water. Before you sterilize soil, put it through a fine sieve. Then wet it down and place it in a covered container in an oven set at 250–350° F for two to three hours. The covering and the low setting are important, because you don't want to burn the organic matter. It will smell, so you might want to minimize the odor by enclosing the whole thing in an oven poultry bag while it's getting the treatment. As an extra precaution, you may want to drench the sterilized soil with a solution of Captan. If you do so, you must wait twenty-four hours before sowing, but the bit of extra trouble can pay off in extra protection against fungi and algae.

The containers, too, should be sterilized before they are filled. Pour boiling water over glass dishes. Plastic can be scrubbed out with a 10 percent Clorox solution.

If you are sowing in simple sterilized soil or a mix that includes it, let it cool down before spooning it into your containers. Whatever mix you use, fill the containers only to within an inch of the top; the young ferns will need headroom for growing. Except when you're sowing or watering, you must keep the sterile medium covered at all times.

A word about watering: use only distilled or boiled water. Tap water contains too many algae and moss spores and could mean annihilation. Large, well-established plants can handle these contaminants, but tender young gametophytes and germinating spores may be wiped out or crowded out. Water the medium well and you are ready for sowing.

Sowing.   Have everything ready before you lay a hand on your first packet of spores—and open only one at a time.

Spores are so light in weight that when you unveil them they're likely to do what nature designed them to do—float off on air. You can reduce inadvertent combinations by sowing only one kind of fern at a time, or even sowing different kinds in different rooms, if you have enough space. No matter how careful you are, though, some spores will almost inevitably land in dishes not destined for them. Don't be surprised at the mavericks that eventually pop up.

The best way to get spores evenly distributed is to sprinkle them out of their container onto one of those invaluable sheets of white paper, uncover the planting dish, turn the paper upside-down over it, and tap. The spores cling to the paper until your tapping dislodges them. If this seems too chancy for an inexperienced sower to try, simply uncover your dish and gently tap the spores out of their capsule or envelope so that they fall evenly over the surface. You want them as well distributed as possible—they should not be jammed into the dish or pot. A few will go a long way; too many will choke one another out as they grow.

The moment the spores are distributed, re-cover the dish. From beginning to end, you want it exposed to the air for the absolute minimum of time.

You probably don't need to worry about watering for quite a while. Check periodically to make sure the dish does not completely dry out. Even if it does dry out, you may be able to rescue your gametophytes by adding water, unless they've been dehydrated for too long. It's always worth a try. However, be careful not to overwater. The air in the dish should have 100 percent humidity, but the medium should never be soggy or show standing water.

As you finish sowing each dish, label it with a small piece of paper taped to the outside, listing the species, the date,

Top: Sowing spores onto soil.
Bottom: A plastic shoebox of young ferns.
The pots are full of prothalli, and the pale fronds
of young ferns can be seen.

and anything else that seems worth recording. You may think you're going to remember all these details, but one never does.

Light. Try for a north or east window. Never place the dishes where strong, direct sunlight will reach them. Rays like these can bring the dish's interior temperature to over 100° F, literally cooking the young plantlets. On the other hand, don't listen to anyone who advises you to select a dark spot for germination. The spores require light to get going, and later on the young plants need light for good growth. It's only the sun's direct, blistering rays you want to avoid.

Artificial light is actually better than natural light when you're working with spores. It can be stronger and yet better controlled, both in intensity and duration. Fourteen to eighteen hours of light per day is perfectly acceptable; in fact, no dark period at all is required. I kept some cultures under a fluorescent desk lamp for two years, and they flourished. You don't need any sort of fancy setup—a single fluorescent tube about 8 inches above your planting dish will give excellent results. A strip of cheesecloth or green cellophane placed over the dish can be helpful in cutting down the growth of unwanted algae.

growth and development

The age of the spores, the variety of fern, and the medium used for sowing all affect the time it will take for the spores to germinate. In general, fresh spores sown on water will germinate in one to two weeks. If they are sown on other media and kept well moistened, look for them in two to three weeks. Some species are slower. Some staghorns, for example, can take up to a year.

If you want to know exactly when germination first occurs, check often with your magnifying lens. The earliest signs of life are imperceptible to the naked eye. However, perhaps a month after sowing, you'll note that the surface of your planting dish is tinted with green. This is it: the spores have germinated and sent out their early filamentous growth. Then, as the filaments begin to broaden to form the prothalli, the young gametophytes become crowded, overlapping and even holding each other upright. This is when you appreciate why, earlier on, I cautioned against packing your dish with too many spores, minute though they are. When they're fresh and well treated, crowds of them germinate; you'll rarely see space between them.

Prothalli, complete with antheridia and archegonia, may be mature in one to three months. At some point they will stop growing. This signals that they have reached their full size, and you will soon see young fern plantlets—young sporophytes—arising from the notches of the prothalli. Each prothallus produces only one such plantlet. Evidently, once fertilization has taken place, a message goes out through the little structure to cease any further generative activity.

If the prothalli appear to have reached maturity but produce no plantlets, the chances are that the culture is too dry for fertilization to have taken place. If there is not enough free water to help the sperms along, they don't reach their objectives. Lend a hand by sprinkling or misting the gametophytes with distilled or boiled and cooled water. If there's still no action after a couple of weeks, try again. All else being equal, water is bound to make the difference.

When the young fiddleheads appear, let them become established, with a few roots and a few leaves each, before transplanting them to larger quarters. Even when you judge

95

that the moment for transplanting has come, don't try to separate out individual plantlets. The roots suffer less disturbance if you prick out a little clump at a time and transplant to a larger pot, a small flat, or a terrarium. If your new container is to include more than one clump, keep at least an inch between them. Try to maintain the conditions they had in their first home, including 100 percent humidity, until they reach about an inch in height. Be sure they have good drainage (a terrarium must have a layer of gravel at the bottom). The soil in the transplant container should be the same soil/leaf mold/sand mixture that you will later use for the mature plants.

When the plantlets attain their inch, they are ready to become individual plants. Separate each of them out and replant in rows in a terrarium or large pot until they grow 2 or more inches tall. Then set them in individual 2-inch pots. This is probably the most critical period for spore-

Young fronds of a maidenhair fern.

raised ferns. They're on their own, but still dependent on the careful treatment they've been getting, particularly on the high humidity they're used to. They need to be accustomed gradually to the outside world, especially to the lower humidity of the average home. Don't be in a hurry to get the 2-inch pots onto your window sill. I keep mine for a couple of months in a kind of nursery with sides and a top, propping the top an inch or two up so that the harsh air of the real world can mix gradually with the plants' original deluxe environment. A terrarium with a top that can be opened is a good choice. Many gardeners are successful with fish tanks topped with glass slabs that can be propped open.

Earlier, I mentioned water as a sowing medium. It has a few advantages, one being that it helps spores to germinate faster than when sown on solid media. The process is much the same: both the container and the water that fills it must be sterilized. When you sprinkle the spores on the surface, don't worry about the few that sink. Most will float and germinate. When the gametophytes mature—when they have stopped growing— they can be spooned out onto soil, into small depressions an inch or so apart. Wait until the fiddleheads of young ferns appear, then thin and transplant as described above.

problems and pests

Mold is your enemy. It comes in on the fern sporangia, and even from the air itself. It can be controlled by the application of a very weak solution of copper sulfate (1 part per 10 million) or of potassium permanganate, which should be just barely purple.

Algae may also attack. These, from the water or soil, are

98

Transplanting baby staghorn ferns from the spore-growing pot into a larger pot to provide growing space.

not so easily controlled. In the young stages, they appear as branching green threads; then they become greenish-black slime and mosses, which must be removed with tweezers. Sometimes a solution of Algex will control an algal invasion that's not too overpowering. Generally, though, once it gets going you either have to throw out the whole pot or hope that the gametophytes will survive long enough to get the sporophytes on their way. When they are old enough to be moved, transplanting them into sterile new pots and soil may help.

Minute animals in the soil can be controlled by applying dilute water-soluble sevin.

All these controls are emergency measures. Do your best to avoid needing them by using sterile soil, containers, and water, and observing the precautions about giving the spores as little exposure to air as possible when you're handling them.

special equipment

You really don't need any. Certainly no fancy tools are required. Tweezers are handy for separating young plants; keep a separate pair for removing algae (and hope you won't have to use them). A vegetable peeler is another handy gadget. One digs with the gently curving tip and tamps down with the handle. A long aluminum gutter nail can be used in the same way: the point for making planting holes, the head end for tamping the soil. Lobster picks have also been known to come in handy. The two-tined end is used for cutting and dividing, and the small scoop for lifting the young ferns.

5.

**growing your own:
by vegetative means**

as we have seen, the spore is historically and botanically fascinating, but a bit of a loser when it comes to the practical activities of fern reproduction. Most of the ferns that have survived and flourished through the ages owe their success to their capacity to reproduce by an additional means: vegetative.

Many fern plants—most, in fact—can reproduce vegetatively. This simply means that the parent plant produces offspring from some part of itself that is neither seed nor spore. With ferns in the wild, vegetative reproduction usually occurs when some part either breaks off and roots, or forms buds that go on to become new plants. In cultivation, with this method of propagation new plants can be obtained anywhere from instantly to within a few months, faster than by spore propagation at its best.

The simplest form of vegetative reproduction comes about in nature when the rhizome branches. Besides producing new leaves and roots, the rhizome also develops branch buds, which grow out laterally to form clumps. This is how widely creeping species like the bracken and the hay-scented fern expand to cover whole hillsides, clearings, even sizable meadows. As the branches continue to grow, the rhizome gradually dies off at its older end, and the branches separate from one another. You can speed up the process by merely breaking off a rooted branch and replanting it. Even crown-forming ferns may branch to form small plants around their bases. By carefully breaking these off and planting them separately, you achieve an instant garden in the easiest, and least expensive, way possible.

In addition to reproducing
by spores, many ferns also propagate
themselves vegetatively.

Top: This pot of *Asplenium cuspidatum* is being
divided by simply breaking apart the mass
of branched rhizomes. Bottom: The rhizome of this
squirrel's-foot fern is being cut and
planted separately to form a new plant.

The interesting footed ferns (squirrel's-foot, rabbit's-foot, and so on) can be readily multiplied. Cut off the terminal 4 to 6 inches of a "foot" and replant it. If it is well rooted, it should take off at once. If not, you will need to pin it down to the soil until roots form; this can take several weeks. You can get such plants started by using a technique known as air-layering. Pack moist sphagnum moss around the rhizome a few inches back from the tip, wrap the arrangement in plastic, and tie it in place. Wrapped this way, roots will form quickly. Once roots do form, cut the rooted tip from the parent plant, clean away the sphagnum, and plant.

In some plants, such as the ostrich fern and some species of *Blechnum*, the side branches are particularly long and slender. These runners, or stolons, are responsible for the

A rhizome of the rabbit's-foot fern being "air-layered." Moist sphagnum wrapped in plastic encourages roots to form so the rhizome can be divided and planted.

appearance of young plants some distance away from the
parent rhizome. The new plants are the products of the
parent plant's subterranean stolons, which push out through
the ground to do their generative work. The young develop
their own roots. You can turn them into individual plants by
carefully cutting through their attachment to the parent.

The most conspicuous example of stolons occurs in the
Boston fern and its relatives, the genus *Nephrolepis*, in the
form of long, slender, hairlike strings that grow among the
leaves. These strings bear tiny buds, and when pinned down
to the soil they will form a chain of new plants along their
whole length. In a greenhouse bench they will root readily
in the moist gravel around the pot. This is an easy way of
propagating the varieties of *Nephrolepis* that frequently do
not produce spores.

In some groups of ferns the roots themselves form buds,
which grow stem and leaves and start to produce their own

Stolons from the
Boston fern produce babies if
they touch the soil.

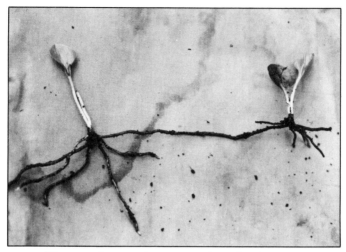

roots. The epiphytic spleenworts that do this often have crowds of young plants around them. The adder's-tongue (*Ophioglossum*) also produces root buds, but these may be so far away from the parent plant that one has to dig them up before the root connections become apparent. One cultivated species, *Ophioglossum petiolatum*, is a particularly satisfactory performer, filling a pot very quickly with root proliferations.

Staghorn ferns are another group that form root buds, and as one might expect, these eccentric-looking plants also proliferate eccentrically. Most of these *Platycerium* species grow roots long enough to get the young, which are called pups, out from under the shield leaves of the parent. They can be seen along the margins of the cabbagelike shield leaves, developing into new, though still attached, plantlets. When their leaves are 2 to 3 inches long, use a sharp knife to cut under the shield frond and well into the rooting me-

The adder's-tongue
fern multiplies rapidly from
buds on the roots.

108

Staghorns produce "pups"
from their roots. These can be
removed and replanted.

dium to slice out the rooted portion of the pup, and a new set of antlers will be on its way.

Plantlets also develop on the surface of the leaf in some plants, which are called "mother ferns." The babies may be so abundant that the leaf droops to the ground. Sometimes they drop off on their own and root, as happens with the Mauritius mother-fern (*Asplenium daucifolium*) and the Oriental chain fern (*Woodwardia orientalis*); or they can be picked off and easily rooted in peat or moist soil. In the common mother-fern (*Asplenium bulbiferum*) the young are more stubborn. They develop their own leaves, yet remain firmly attached to the mother leaf even as it lies on the ground. They may not free themselves until it has actually disintegrated. If you want to speed them toward independence, pin the mother leaf to the soil. The youngsters will root more quickly and be ready to make their own way.

The bulblet bladder-fern (*Cystopteris bulbifera*) illustrates another kind of bud reproduction: the main rachis and major lateral veins produce large round buds that fall off easily, like little seeds or beads. The buds look like round beans with a large fleshy lobe on either side of the growing tip. In the greenhouse or in the wild, hundreds of young are found beneath plants of this species, the result of this vegetative fall-off. The halberd mother-fern (*Tectaria gemmifera*) similarly produces quantities of hard, buttonlike buds, in this case on the upper surfaces of the rachis and veins. A five-year-old specimen in our greenhouse has so far generated literally thousands of young plants. The new plants keep showing up for months after we have moved the parent to another spot.

Altogether, bud reproduction is one of the most reliable and interesting ways ferns have developed for keeping **109**

110

Top: *Diplazium proliferum* produces
babies in the axils of the leaflets. Bottom:
The Mauritius mother-fern bears babies
on the upper surface of the frond.

themselves going, and it occurs in many diverse forms. One striking means is by the rooting of an extended rachis: the rachis of the leaf grows on well beyond the last pinnae, and on contact with the soil produces a baby plant. This in turn develops leaves with extended tips that go on to repeat the rooting process, so that the offshoots of the plant appear to be walking across the forest floor. There are many examples of this habit in the spleenworts and their close relatives, but it occurs in other groups as well. The North American walking fern is a familiar example. Another is the walking maidenhair (*Adiantum caudatum*) of southern Asia.

In certain ferns, buds appear along the leaf margins. When the star-shaped leaf of the strawberry fern touches the ground, or when the plant is growing in high humidity, buds often develop in the leaf notches. If you pin a strawberry fern's leaf to the soil, you will soon have an exciting harvest. I have seen as many as thirty-five buds develop on a single leaf treated in this manner.

The halberd mother-fern
bears buds that fall off to
form new plants.

111

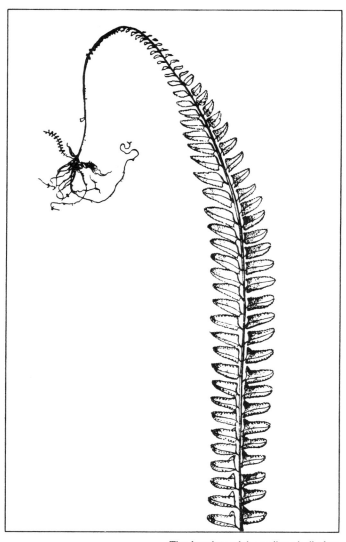

112

The frond tip of the walking holly fern
(*Polystichum maximowiczii*) is elongated
and roots to form a new plant.

You can also work a bit of magic with a plant like *Asplenium exiguum*, which is capable of forming buds at the tips of all its pinnae. Under normal conditions in the wild, the buds don't develop, since *A. exiguum* is native to relatively dry regions of the Himalayas, Mexico, and the southwestern United States. However, if you can capture one of the plants in the high humidity of a bottle garden or terrarium, you will have the peculiar satisfaction of going nature one better. You will see the vegetative buds developing, forming a necklace of young around each leaf. Like other bud-producing fronds, these need only be pinned to the ground to get the buds rooted and on to maturity.

Many other ferns proliferate through bud reproduction. The fronds of some of the holly ferns (*Polystichum*) and *Diplazium proliferum* are usually loaded with potential new

The strawberry fern
(*Hemionitis palmata*) bears a baby
in a notch in the frond.

113

plants. The European chain fern (*Woodwardia radicans*) does it a little differently: it produces a single large bud near the tip of the rachis, which develops rapidly as soon as the frond tip becomes so heavy that it bends down to the soil. In the hand fern (*Doryopteris pedata*) the buds are restricted to the base of the blade and grow into plantlets only under heavily humid conditions. The European hart's-tongue is also a little reluctant, though capable of bud production. You can induce it to develop plantlets on the leaf stalk by cutting off and planting tender young leaves.

There is still another reproductive trick that appears to be the exclusive secret of the primitive genus *Marattia* and its relatives. So far as we know, it is only in this family of large tropical plants that swellings, or lateral growths, develop at the leaf bases. They are called stipules, and when the leaves die they fall off just above these stipules, which apparently remain to protect the rhizomes. The accumulation of stipules and old leaf bases can make a rhizome appear several inches thick, when in reality it is only about the thickness of a finger. Removed from the stem and planted, each stipule becomes a new plant. In fact, if you cut one in half, you will get a new plant from each piece.

In recent years professionals have developed a technique of tissue culture that greatly speeds up the production of new plants. It is based on the fern's ability to reproduce vegetatively, and the aim is to culture a small piece of the plant tissue to make it develop several growing points, which are then separated and encouraged to form new plants. Any growing part of the plant, such as a stem tip or crosier, is cut off, sterilized, and placed on a special nutrient agar, a jellylike substance in which nutrients and vitamins have been dissolved. After about five weeks roots form; the tip is then transferred to another agar enriched with hormones that will promote multiplication. After five weeks in this second medium, the single tip will have multiplied to produce many small plants. These are separated, hardened by exposure to stronger light, and then planted individually or recultured to produce more growing tips. Thus a single plant becomes the source of many more offspring than it could produce on its own, and mature plants are obtained more quickly than would be possible through spore culture.

In a more complicated process, the same technique is applied to the gametophyte generation, the prothalli. Sterilized spores, sown on nutrient agar, grow rapidly into prothalli, which are then macerated in a blender with additional nutrients and hormones. When this mixture is poured onto sterile soil, each prothallus fragment can be counted on to develop into a mature prothallus. The resulting plants develop quickly. This technique is especially useful when spore material is limited. Obviously, though, it is not very practical for the amateur, who is not likely to have the time or the necessary equipment.

But this is small loss. For the average fern enthusiast, the vegetative magic the plant itself can perform—perhaps with just a little help in the matter of cutting off and replanting— is surely exciting and rewarding enough.

6.

indoor cultivation

do ferns make good house plants? I have to admit that the only good answer is a hedge: it depends. It depends on the fern, and it depends on the house. Some ferns come indoors quite cooperatively, others will not make it without an impractical amount of coddling, and there are some that should never be asked, not even when you can offer a greenhouse.

The fact is that we are far from knowing all that we might about cultivating ferns. The experience we've so far collected, about 150-odd years' worth, is limited to comparatively few species. In 1813 there were thirty species under cultivation in the Berlin Botanic Garden, and eighty species being grown in England—botanically speaking, not much of a spread. But a Victorian fern craze was about to be triggered by two interesting developments.

In the 1840s the English botanist Nathaniel Bagshaw Ward discovered that plants could be grown in specially designed closed cases, which meant that even a modest household could take a chance with a plant that previously could have been nurtured only in a greenhouse. Shortly afterward, in 1852, scientists clarified the fact that ferns can be propagated by spores, and that in the fern's life history the spore-producing, or sporophyte, generation is followed by the gametophyte generation, a process (often referred to as the alternation of generations) that we looked at in Chapter 3. Ferns from remote lands began to swarm into England, joining the other exotica flourishing in the "Wardian cases" that sprang up everywhere.

The Boston fern (*Nephrolepis exaltata* var. *Bostoniensis*) is the all-time favorite fern in cultivation.

It was some years before fern cultivation caught on in North America. The plant that first captured the public interest was the Boston fern, a variety of *Nephrolepis exaltata*, one of the sword ferns. Actually this species had been in cultivation for some time, a rather unremarkable plant generating little excitement. But around 1894 it suddenly began producing longer, more decorative fronds. An accidental mutation had taken place, one of the random genetic changes that occur rather frequently in plants without attracting much notice. It simply happened that the Boston fern's change was so marked and attractive that growers began to propagate it with enthusiasm, and they have hardly stopped since. They already knew that it had one vital qualification as a house plant: it would survive. It came from the right environment.

ferns from the right families

We cannot cultivate any plant, indoors or out, until we have paid respectful attention to its environment in the wild. With ferns, the most important single environmental factor is humidity. The majority of the world's ferns come from humid regions, primarily tropical forests. Whether they grow on the forest floor or occur as epiphytes on tree trunks and branches, they receive abundant moisture in the form of rain or fog. The relative humidity in such areas generally ranges from 70 to 100 percent. In contrast, the humidity in the average home is about 25 percent. This is a dramatic difference, and while some ferns turn out to be less thirsty and more adaptable than others, there are relatively few that can withstand the constant low humidity of most home environments.

The ferns that will do well indoors, even with humidity

on the low side, are generally tropical epiphytes. Like terrestrial ferns, they come from warm, damp climates, but they live above the ground, and their tree habitats can sometimes become temporarily dry. This doesn't happen in cloud forests and most rain forests, where the moisture is so constant that nothing ever dries out. There are other forests, though, in which the rain is not so regular, and the rains that do fall run off down the trees. Plants up above may be exposed to fairly frequent dry periods, and only those that can withstand such irregular watering will survive.

The tropical *Nephrolepis* species sometimes occur on the ground, but most frequently they are epiphytes, occurring on tree trunks and branches. Of the thirty or so different kinds, some are less than a foot high, others so tall that their long, pendent fronds sweep downward for as much as 8 feet. In Guatemala I saw one dramatic species, the pendulous sword fern (*N. pendula*), being cultivated in high-hanging baskets. The 6- to 10-foot fronds, drooping lushly toward the floor, are called *cola de quetzal* because of their resemblance to the long, green, pendulous tail of the quetzal bird.

The Boston fern, then, came from a family accustomed to a spot of dryness now and then, and that made it a prime candidate for indoor cultivation when it did its Cinderella act and turned pretty, as it were, overnight. Since that first happy accident, it has undergone many mutations, probably more than any other cultivated fern, and from these mutations growers have developed hundreds of different forms. It may be that some of the "new" forms are really repeats of earlier, forgotten varieties, because little work has been done in the way of standardizing and verifying what is truly new. But all the Boston fern variations available are ap-

121

The pendulous sword fern has fronds up to 10 feet long.

pealing and quite durable, and that's what matters to the home gardener. Instead of being only once-divided, as *Nephrolepis* originally was, the new varieties are two, three, even four times divided, making for very delicate, feathery fronds. Some of the long, open types hang out of their containers like lengths of fragile lace. Others are quite different: short, compact, upright, though still feathery. If you look for varieties like Fluffy Ruffles, Irish Lace, Ruffled Petticoat, and Emerald Fleece, you'll see at once how they got their names.

Another plus for Bostons is that they are easy to reproduce. The many-dissected forms do not produce spores, so they must reproduce vegetatively. Like all *Nephrolepis*, they use their stolons for the purpose. Anyone who owns one Boston can easily acquire a family by pinning the stolons down to the soil (see Chapter 5). This is why, though Boston ferns do well in pots, baskets are probably a better place for them. The stolons will run through the soil and send out young plants through the sides of the basket, creating a very pretty effect.

Every now and then a many-dissected *Nephrolepis* will send up an out-of-character leaf, divided only once instead of many times like its neighbors. Don't worry about this. The plant isn't ailing. And don't get overexcited about the possibility that you have stumbled on a new variety. What you have is simply an accidental throwback to the ancestral form, the simple once-divided leaf. Cutting off the upstart at once will discourage the plant from playing any more tricks of reversion, and remind it that it is currently in the business of producing multidivided fronds. You don't want your Cinderella to change back into a plain Jane.

A word about watering. I have said that the many forms

of *N. exaltata* do well indoors because they're used to occasional periods of less-than-ideal humidity. This doesn't mean that they will survive irregular watering. They won't. Unless they are watered frequently and regularly, their roots will dry out and the fronds will turn brown. The plant will not give up completely until it is neglected for so long that it loses all hope, but it will struggle along, half alive, waving increasing numbers of brown fronds at you in a desperate effort to remind you of your responsibility. When you see such browning, immediately step up your watering schedule. As you revive the plant, remove the discolored fronds. If you're beginning to do the right thing, new green ones will eventually replace them.

Face facts. If you know you can't count on yourself to meet a regular watering deadline, adopt a plant that can tolerate a little dryness. The tuberous sword fern (*Nephrolepis cordifolia*) will make it. This is a rigidly erect or slightly arching plant, with fronds generally once-divided, though some varieties are twice-cut. The pinnae tend to overlap slightly. It takes more than irregular watering to discourage this one. I don't suggest that you go out of your way to abuse it, but it is a fact that however irregular the watering—the pot may become bone dry—the tuberous sword's fronds remain erect and the young crosiers rise stiff and uncurling. Also, the plant makes do with less light than is needed by *N. exaltata*.

Another fern that offers a lot of interest and decorative value in return for very little pampering is the staghorn, of the genus *Platycerium*. There are only eighteen species in this genus—most of them native to southeast Asia and Africa, one from South America—but many more cultivars. Staghorns are distinguished by having two kinds of

Top: Many varieties of the Boston
fern are very finely divided.
Bottom: *Platycerium bifurcatum* is the most
commonly cultivated staghorn.

fronds: cabbagelike shield leaves that hug the trunk on which the plant grows, and spreading, arching, forking fronds that carry on most of the food manufacture and spore production. With their sometimes eerie resemblance to a stag's antlers, staghorns are not what most plant-lovers call beautiful, but curious and fascinating they certainly are. And for the lackadaisical gardener they're a bonanza, for they are very nearly as hardy as they look. They need to be watered only once a week. In a pinch they can go dry even longer. I have gone on vacation and left mine for as long as three weeks with no ill effects. The fronds may eventually go a little limp in protest, but they perk right up again the moment you soak the soil. There is more danger of overwatering than of underwatering.

Because of their bizarre forms, staghorns are popular indoors not only as plants but as decorative accessories. They can be handsomely and fairly easily mounted on plaques of any sort of wood that will not rot with watering, redwood and cedar shingles being particularly good. I have seen them attractively attached to driftwood and to cork slabs. I have even seen one centered in a wall-hung automobile air filter, though I think this is probably an acquired taste.

This kind of mounting is possible because the staghorn does not need to be planted in soil. It generally comes from the nursery in a small pot or small ball of sphagnum or fern fiber (tree-fern or osmunda fiber). To mount it, lay your plaque flat, and on it form a nest of sphagnum. Adding a little well-rotted sheep manure won't hurt. In the middle, place the plant with its root ball. Pull the surrounding planting medium up around this and tie the whole thing in place with colorless fishing line or plastic-coated wire. Hang the plaque near a window. Watering, which is necessary only once or twice a week, is best accomplished by soaking the whole arrangement in the bathtub for a few minutes. Staghorns vary somewhat with the various species. The one you see most often is *Platycerium bifurcatum*, whose fairly dark green leaves are covered with a light coating of minute star-shaped hairs. *Platycerium veitchii*, less common, is very pale, with an extremely dense hair covering. The most spectacular are *P. superbum*, *P. grande*, and *P. holttumii*. All have very large fronds. The forking fronds grow several feet long and the shield leaves sweep upward, with jagged margins that give the plant an almost menacing look. In some species the veins of the shield leaves stand out like the ridges of a waffle iron.

A whole wall of staghorns looks rather eerie, and understandably there is a vast body of collectors fascinated by their strangeness whose goal is to acquire examples of every possible variation. It seems feasible because the total is relatively small, but before you acquire an addiction to staghorns keep in mind that not all species are easy to housebreak. Some are rare. Some are difficult to grow. To try for a complete collection is to take on a real challenge.

In addition, because of the world-wide demand for staghorns, they are being collected extensively—and often carelessly—in the wild, so that natural populations are diminishing. If you are drawn to them, try growing the rarer ones from spores. It takes more time, but you will be helping to preserve threatened species. *Platycerium* does not produce the neat, small sori typical of most ferns. If your plant is *P. bifurcatum*, look for the spores in patches near the ends of the forking fronds. In some species the fertile patches are in a notch between the forkings. In others a special lobe forms to bear the sporangia.

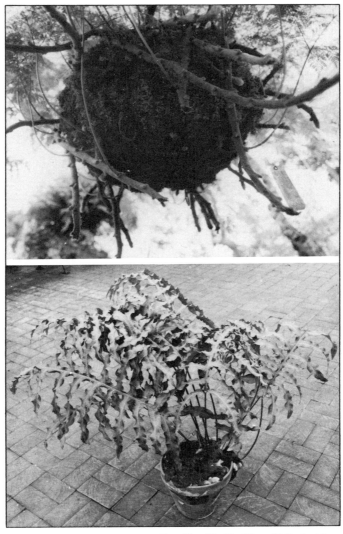

Top: The "feet" of the rabbit's-foot fern
are scaly, long-creeping rhizomes.
Bottom: The arching fronds of the golden
polypody may grow to 4 feet long.

Easier to grow, and very popular, are the so-called footed ferns. Their creeping rhizomes, covered with conspicuous scales in colors ranging from orange to gray or white, bear some resemblance to the animal feet for which they are named—though as I indicated earlier, the names squirrel's-foot, deer's-foot, rabbit's-foot, and so on are casually used and often interchangeable.

Being animal-footed doesn't prevent these ferns from displaying true ferny charm. *Davallias*, for example, develop fronds of the most delicate laciness, divided four to six times, each ultimate segment consisting of scarcely more than the essential midvein with a slender greenness on either side. These, generally called rabbit's-foot, are outstanding basket plants, with rhizomes that creep and branch over the surface of the soil and thrust out through the sides of the basket to make a huge ball. At Longwood Gardens near Philadelphia there is one marvelous specimen that makes a basket nearly 10 feet in diameter. *Davallia* fronds are generally about 2 feet long and gently arching, but there are smaller forms as well. The rhizome scales are tan or brown—rabbit-colored enough to make the plant identifiable by its common name.

Closely related to *Davallia* is *Humata*, the squirrel's-foot fern. The species most likely to be available is *H. tyermannii*, which looks much like *Davallia* but has fronds only 8 to 12 inches long. Its rhizome scales are white and more slender than those of *Davallia*. For some purposes it can be a better choice. While it will never achieve the spectacular size of the rabbit's-foot, its rhizomes creep quickly to hang over the sides of a basket and you can soon work up a creditable ball by pinning them down against the basket's outer surface. You might consider making a project out of *Humata*, since of the fifty known species there are several that we suspect would make good house plants if enough serious fern fanciers took the trouble to try them. This is how the boundaries of indoor gardening are stretched.

Another footed fern candidate is the bear's-foot, or golden polypody (*Polypodium aureum*). The several forms of this all have stout creeping rhizomes covered with spreading, bright orange scales. If you concentrate on *P. aureum*, you can assemble quite a varied display. Some are compact, with fronds only a foot tall. Others have fronds that arch outward to 4-foot lengths. Nearly all the fronds are once-divided. Colors range from yellow-green to an odd blue with a kind of whitish bloom on the surface. The pinnae may be smooth-margined like the wild type, or ruffled- or cut-margined as in the varieties *mandianum* and *tessellata*. Polypody sori are easy to spot: round and orange, they make a neat row down either side of the pinna midvein. Since polypody occurs in the wild both on the ground and on trees, it does well in either a pot or a hanging basket.

One of my personal indoor favorites is the bird's-nest— usually labeled *Asplenium nidus*, though it may actually be one of several different species of *Asplenium* sold under that name. Its broad, upright, glossy leaves make an impressive show, and it is quite tolerant of even harsh home conditions. It bears up bravely under infrequent watering. Only when dryness becomes really severe does it protest by going limp. The fronds never turn brown, no matter how dehydrated it becomes. Direct sunlight will burn it, and rubbing against hard objects will damage its edges, but if you protect it from these hazards, it will reward you by forming a beautiful plant as much as 2 or even 3 feet tall. The leaves, narrow or broad, rise sharply in some forms. Others curve outward at the base before rising, forming a distinct bowl.

Top: The glossy leaves of the
bird's-nest fern are especially attractive.
Bottom: The button fern takes its name from
its round blackish-green leaflets.

In their native areas in southeast Asia and the South Pacific, *Asplenium* fronds will grow 5 feet long, making dramatic "bird's nests" on the trunks of their supporting trees.

Going by the environmental guidelines I offered earlier, if you're looking for ferns to be set on a floor or window sill, it's best to select from those that are basically terrestrial in the wild. One such group is *Pellaea*. The green cliff-brake (*Pellaea viridis*), an African native (also called *P. adiantoides*), is a handsome plant about a foot tall, with a noticeably dark purplish-brown leaf stalk and dark green foliage, once- or twice-divided. The sori, black when ripe, appear along the margins of the leaflets. You might also check out *P. rotundifolia*, the widely available button fern— a good example of how far a fern can travel from the popular notion of ferniness. *Pellaea rotundifolia*'s 6- to 8-inch fronds, hanging over their pot rims, are threaded with double rows of round, plump little leaflets that look very much like solid dark green buttons: very striking, but far from airy. *Pellaeas* adapt well enough to normal household humidity, but they do need more consistent watering than *Polypodiums* and *Aspleniums*. Also, you should be on the alert for scale insects. *Pellaeas* are particularly susceptible; they will be among the first to get scale and the last to shake it off, however knowledgeably you help.

From the genus *Pteris* come several attractive candidates. Commonly known as brakes, or table ferns, they show up in several varieties that have interesting form and shading. The Cretan brake (*Pteris cretica*) ranges from 1 to 3 feet tall, from dark green to light, and in the variety *Albolineata* has a white band down the center of each pinna. This Asian native is widely cultivated, and in some warm regions it has escaped to grow wild as a pantropic weed. More color can be added to your fern garden with the Victorian brake (*P. ensiformis* var. *victoriae*), whose slender pinnae are edged with dark green leaflets centered with white. Another worth looking for is the spider brake (*P. multifida*), named for its particularly long, slender pinnae and pinnules.

For more striking color, find members of the genus *Pityrogramma*—the silverback (*P. calomelanos*) and goldback (*P. hybrida*) ferns. The distinctive color created by wax glands on the leaf undersides—white in *calomelanos*, bright gold in *hybrida*—is occasionally diluted by the sporangia, which are pepper-dotted among the glands.

Spectacular, but somewhat more demanding, are the climbing ferns. To domesticate these, you need to provide more humidity than is necessary for the genera already discussed, but the results are worth the trouble. One popular species, the Japanese climbing fern (*Lygodium japonicum*), has rhizomes that spread over the surface of the ground, with each frond unrolling gradually in a seemingly never-ending process. There are two in my home that have reached 8 feet in height, but they're slackers in comparison with some grown by my friend Dr. Barbara McMartin. Hers have gone 18 feet up a post in a stairwell.

A climbing fern needs strings or wires for support and guidance, but once it gets the drift of the direction you want it to take, it rolls (or unrolls) right along until the food supply or the size of the rhizome calls a natural halt. If you don't have a tall post like Dr. McMartin's on which your fern can develop to its utmost, fasten the strings around a window or doorway. The plant will grow where you lead it and gradually become a handsome frame. Give each frond its own string or wire to travel. This shows all the growth off to best advantage and makes grooming easier. If a frond

133

134

The twining fronds of the
Japanese climbing fern quickly take
advantage of any support.

dies it can be easily removed without interfering with neigh-boring fronds, with which it would otherwise be entwined. When aging or dead fronds are not removed the plant starts to look shabby, so it's wise to keep old and new fronds from intermingling.

coping with humidity

If you're ambitious to grow ferns other than those already discussed, prepare to deal seriously with the humidity factor. This doesn't have to be as difficult as it sounds. As we've seen, most of the ferns that originate in tropical forests don't absolutely require a constant humidity of 90 to 100 percent, and those that do are not readily available anyway. A green-house—there are now several small practical ones on the market—will eliminate most problems by supplying humid-ity of 60 to 70 percent, but even without one don't assume you're out of the fern business. If you can get your indoor humidity up to 40 or 50 percent, a wide variety of ferns will be happy to settle in with you, and fortunately there are a number of relatively simple ways by which humidity can be boosted indoors.

Your first approach might be to try a commercially avail-able humidifier, either set in one room or attached to the furnace to raise humidity throughout the house. In the right circumstances these can work wonders. Sometimes, how-ever, you will need a greater, more concentrated increase for a very small area. An easy way to achieve this—one that I have used with great success—is with a pebble tray. In a rustproof tray, make a shallow bed of gravel (pea gravel or marble chips serve well). Fill the tray with water to just below the top of the gravel, then set the plants on it. No water should touch the pot bottoms. By keeping the water level in the tray constant, you can keep the air around it at a humidity range of 50 to 70 percent. There is also a bonus: plants grouped together, as they are on such trays, raise the humidity around them with the moisture they themselves give off.

For higher humidity and more constant conditions, it's not difficult to construct a mini-greenhouse, a simple chamber that can be equipped with lights. I have done this with strips of 2-by-2-inch lumber cut and nailed together to make a frame 2 feet deep, 4 feet long, and 30 inches high. Covered on all sides with plastic, this makes an excellent greenhouse, which can be kept wherever there is enough space to install two 4-foot white fluorescent lights just above it. A removable front panel allows ample access to the plants inside, or perhaps you can simply arrange the front plastic flap to fold back at need. Line the bottom of the frame with an extra piece of heavyweight plastic and cover this with a 2-inch bed of peat or sphagnum moss, which is to be kept quite moist—just short of soggy—at all times, thus keeping the humidity at a constant high. This is an excellent spot for small plants in pots or baskets; young plants can be weaned here as well. Give them about fourteen hours of light per day. You'll find that your ferns shed spores here readily, and baby plants will volunteer themselves on the moss and even on the sides of pots. The possibilities are limited only by the size of your chamber.

For more decoration and less bulk, you can always fall back on a terrarium. These attractive glass containers add charm to a room without making it obvious that they're really working away to give your plants greenhouse conditions. Since there are plenty of plants to use in terrariums, with more available all the time, it's easy enough to avoid the mistake most often made: filling a terrarium with plants that are acquired when they are babies but will soon be too large for the container. One of my pet peeves is to find "professional" growers, who should know better, selling bottle gardens and terrariums filled with such plants as Boston fern, which will soon outgrow their containers. What you want are plants of the right shape, size, and habit, plants that will remain small and will require only occasional grooming, not all-out landscaping.

To compose a terrarium, first select a practical container. Put in a 1-inch layer of gravel for drainage, a small amount of charcoal to keep the soil from going sour in its enclosed space, and then a couple of inches of sterilized soil. Buy it already sterilized, or sterilize it yourself (see Chapter 4), but don't neglect this requirement. Sterilized soil keeps down the pests, fungi, and mosses that would otherwise multiply and take over. For the rest of your environment, slight variations in terrain and details of landscaping should be added according to your own taste. A few small rocks add a good substrate for ferns.

What is particularly exciting about fern terrariums is that often ferns can be brought in from the wild and nurtured in them. Small species of *Asplenium* are especially promising. One good choice is the maidenhair spleenwort (*Asplenium trichomanes*), which is widespread around the world. It likes rocks, and usually stops growing at 3 to 6 inches. Ebony spleenwort (*Asplenium platyneuron*), with a neat, small rosette of sterile leaves, is another attractive possibility. You can also use some of the spleenworts that make babies at the tips of their fronds or pinnae, like *A. conquisitum* and *A. exiguum*, if you keep in mind that they need to be thinned out quite frequently—but it's a joy to share

137

your bounty and give the overflow away.

Another spreading species that lives well in a terrarium is the walking fern (*Camptosorus rhizophyllus*), with its novel habit of growth, rooting from the tips of its long, slender leaves. The cosmopolitan fragile fern (*Cystopteris fragilis*) and some of the *Woodsias* are useful in spots where you want something upright and delicately cut. If you are using rocks, the small, rock-loving wall rue (*Asplenium rutamuraria*) looks natural with them. *Polystichum tsus-simense*, one of the Japanese holly ferns, is ordinarily a house plant but can be kept small enough for a terrarium. Maidenhairs, which need high humidity, are natural candidates. Investigate the rosy maidenhair (*Adiantum hispidulum*) among others. The hand fern (*Doryopteris pedata*) and the strawberry fern (*Hemionitis palmata*) are both small and star-shaped and will add interesting variety of form.

For ground cover, try some of the spikemosses (*Selaginella*). There are more than six hundred species, so there are sure to be some available. The species *S. kraussiana* spreads very quickly, which may be an asset in some cases. If you need something shorter-creeping and more erect, try the tree spikemoss (*S. kraussiana* var. *braunii*), with which you can landscape as though it were miniature shrubbery. There are other spikemosses that grow several inches tall, erect as small trees, and there are some with brightly colored leaf undersides or variegated leaves. One or several of them will be invaluable in finishing off your terrarium with professional panache.

Bottle gardens are simply a slight modification of terrariums. There are many beautifully shaped bottles that make excellent homes for small ferns and spikemosses, but often they have narrow necks that make gardening difficult, even

Top: The tree spikemoss is a
good short-creeping form for a bottle garden or
bonsai dish. Bottom: The hand fern has an
interesting frond form.

139

with the special tools that are made for the purpose. It's far better to minimize your headaches by starting with a wide-mouthed container, something you can get your whole hand into. Once planted, your bottle garden will go sailing along practically on its own. I have planted several with mixtures of *Selaginella* species and after an initial watering left them uncapped in narrow-necked bottles for as long as a couple of years—yes, years—without additional watering. The plants fared very well indeed. They did not outgrow the containers, but appeared to reach a balance of growth that was both healthy and consistent with the available space, and altogether created most attractive environments.

As a general rule, the mouth of the terrarium should be covered with a piece of glass, but it should never be sealed off completely. Leaving a crack open to allow slight air movement reduces the chance of molds developing. Even with this small circulation of air, you will need to water your terrarium only once a month, if that often.

Perhaps you yearn for ferns too large for a closed terrarium. No problem. Some of the best, and most easily maintained, gardens under glass are made in fish tanks, which, depending on their size, will take quite large ferns. My friend Dr. David Alsop, who is my kind of indoor gardener—one who believes that less work is more fun and who refuses to be tied to daily watering and plant care—uses old aquariums, 20 gallons or larger. His arrangements sound complicated, but in fact once the materials have been assembled they come together quite logically and simply. Inside the tank, down one corner, attach a length of fairly narrow pipe. Then cut two or three pieces of tubing, each one about 3 inches shorter than the diagonal of the tank. Each piece of tubing should have notches cut into it so that there is an opening every 6 to 8 inches. Attach these "distributor tubes" to the bottom of the vertical pipe in such a way that they radiate out diagonally across the tank bottom. Cover the tank bottom with the same combination you would use for any terrarium: a layer of gravel (2 inches in this case), a layer of charcoal, and sterile soil. Water, about a gallon at a time (depending, of course, on the size of the tank and the number of plants), goes down the corner pipe and spreads out through the distributor tubes into the gravel, so that in effect the plants are watered from below. Most of the water remains in the gravel to become a humidifying reservoir. In this environment your ferns will grow wildly, hanging out over the top and fairly covering the container, often with stunning effect. You will need to water once a month at the most.

The filmy ferns require the ultimate in high humidity, since that's what they get in their natural environment. These may represent more of a challenge than you wish to undertake. First of all, they're hard to find. They're far from widely cultivated. It is difficult to supply the very high humidity they require, though I have seen some in glass jars and closed terrariums. The spores are green and so have a very short life. Also, they are slow to germinate—it can take a year for them to reach the early stages of gametophyte development.

Since you can't readily buy them or propagate them from spores, almost the only way to get hold of filmy ferns is to go out into wet tropical forests and get them yourself. When you do go out to collect them, it is essential that you don't just yank them up. Disturbing them will not make them cooperative. The best technique is to collect a branch or piece of bark on which they are growing. Remove any

141

soil or loose or rotted bark, and any areas where it seems likely that insects might be hiding.

Most of the filmy ferns belong to a single family (Hymenophyllaceae) and are small epiphytes. But there is one from New Zealand that is totally out of character: terrestrial and as much as 2 feet tall. This is the Prince of Wales plume, *Leptopteris superba*. Be warned, however, that in spite of its relatively sturdier look it shares the fragility of its cousins. Like them, it has fronds only one cell thick, and like them it requires very high humidity to survive.

If you should manage to snare any filmy ferns, they can be planted in a combination of sphagnum moss, fir bark, and a touch of soil, or they can be attached to osmunda fiber. Remember the high humidity, and also that they need to be cool—between 50 and 70° F is about right. One good trick is to tie a filmy fern to a brick, then place the brick in a very moist chamber. The brick will transmit moisture at a steady rate to the plant.

how to plant successfully

More often than not, when you acquire a fern to be planted, you get it bare-rooted, or with just a bit of soil around it. Ferns need humidity no matter what stage they're in. You must keep your fledgling moist. Roll it in a towel wrung out of cool water and put the whole thing in a plastic bag until you have assembled all your other planting needs.

First, the container. Whether ornamental or utilitarian, a full-sized pot is too deep for a fern's needs. Fern roots grow very near the surface and don't require a lot of extra space below. Low, fairly shallow pots—about three-quarters to half the depth of full-size pots—are what you want. A pot with a drainage hole is best, but if yours has no hole, put some gravel on the bottom, as you would for any other plant, to hold excess water. If you are using traditional pots, either clay or plastic is satisfactory. Clay dries out more quickly but is perfectly all right so long as you maintain high humidity and water more often than you would with plastic.

As for the soil, there is no single ideal fern mixture. Most important is that it have good drainage—that is, it must not remain soggy after watering—and yet have sufficient water-holding ingredients so that it never dries out. One good combination is equal parts rich soil, compost, peat, and sand. Some growers prefer a combination that contains no soil at all, such as Cornell mix, which is largely peat, vermiculite, and perlite, with added lime and granular fertilizer to provide the necessary minerals. It is also possible to use just peat mixed with sand, relying on liquid fertilizer for nutrients. Whatever the mix, consistency is crucial: when it has been moistened, ready for planting, you should be able to squeeze it and have it hold together fairly well when you release it. It's acceptable if it just barely shows a few cracks. If it remains a globby ball, it will remain soggy in the pot; if it falls apart entirely, it won't hold the moisture the plants need.

When the soil is well mixed and moistened, place a few bits of broken pottery at the bottom of the pot to cover the drainage hole (a small piece of screening or a bit of nylon stocking under the shards will help keep out slugs), and fill the pot halfway up with your planting mix. Make a depression in the center and set the fern in place. Here you must be particularly careful. Unless you are working with a tree fern or a few others with erect rhizomes, do not simply stick in the rhizome vertically. In the wild, most fern rhizomes grow horizontally or at a slight diagonal. Place your rhizome

143

in its shallow nest and, keeping its natural orientation, pack more soil around it. The idea is to set it *on* or just slightly *in* rather than *under* the soil. Few ferns actually grow with buried rhizomes, and what you want to do is imitate nature's way, supporting it in place with soil but not covering it. Most important: even when you place the rhizome horizontally, make sure the growing tip or crown is above the soil level. If it is covered, soil moisture will rot it. Actually, the rhizome will soon work out its own best growing orientation, but why not give it a good start?

When the rhizome is set to your satisfaction, pack it firmly into place, pressing the soil down from the top. Then tap the pot gently on the potting bench to loosen the soil a bit. If you are dealing with a well-grown plant with fronds so large that they threaten to topple the rhizome out of the pot, a couple of U-shaped wires can be used to clip the rhizome into the soil to hold it in place. Water well and place the pot in a shaded, cool, humid place for a few days of adjustment. A plastic bag over the whole thing makes a good humidity-conserving nursery during this period. At potting and re-potting times, humidity is even more important than it is ordinarily, because the roots have been disturbed and cannot supply as much water to the leaves as they are losing.

Pots are far from your only option with ferns. They adapt to baskets of all kinds: wire, wood, coconut fiber, cork. Besides the Bostons and footed ferns that show off at their best in baskets, you might try some of the *Polypodiums*. *Polypodium subauriculatum* cv. *Knightii* is particularly noteworthy. In this variety, the once-divided fronds of the species are deeply cut into long, fine teeth and make a pendulous curtain several feet long. Some small *Polypodiums*, such as *P. piloselloides* and *P. lycopodioides*, make

Top left: The fronds of *Polypodium*
subauriculatum cv. *Knightii* are pendulous and delicately
dissected. Top right: The Victorian brake has variegated fronds.
Bottom: The most commonly cultivated maidenhair fern,
Adiantum raddianum, has many beautiful cultivars.

fine ball ferns when you train and pin the rhizomes around the container as we've already described.

Columns made of chicken wire can be surprisingly easy to make, and most effective. Shape one out of small-mesh wire, line it with sphagnum, and stuff it with a good fern mix. Set it in a dish, which is where the water goes, and plant the ferns along the column sides. Your only problem is to choose plants of a size appropriate for the column.

You may never have aspired to an outdoor rockery, but you can create an indoor one quite easily with ferns. On a bed of moist gravel, set a limestone or tufa rock with cavities of a practical size for holding soil, and then use these cavities as your planting pots.

light

I have read recently in more than one book that ferns are ideal for the cavelike places in your home—dark hallways, dim bathrooms, lightless landings. This, in plain language, is nonsense. Your decorator may want a fern in some such spot, but for the fern itself, it won't do. Ferns need light, strong indirect light. North-facing or east-facing windows are ideal. If you have a skylight, so much the better. Some of the ferns-like-the-dark mythology comes from the fact that they can't tolerate direct, strong sunlight hitting their fronds. This raises their temperature and causes excessive water loss, which dries out the fronds, especially along the edges. They are actually burned by the powerful light. Morning and late-afternoon sunlight is generally not too strong for them, though it is always better when filtered through curtains. In the right kind of light, keep them near your window, not ten feet back.

Your tip-off on inadequate light comes from the condition

of the fronds, just as burned fronds let you know that you've erred at the other end of the scale. What you look for—that is, what you don't want to find—are pale, long, spindly fronds. If it's only the older ones that look like this, don't panic; nature is simply taking its course. But if all the fronds show some of these signs, snap to attention: they're not getting enough light. I was recently shown fronds like this on a plant that, according to what I was told, had been doing well for years, then had suddenly gone limp, yellowish, and spiritless. What had escaped the owner's notice, and what I wasn't told until I asked the right question, was that because of a recent move the plant was now positioned 15 feet from a window. Once it was moved back into the light, it went back on good behavior.

If you don't have good window light, experiment with artificial light. It's not nearly as complicated as you might think. You won't even need special plant-growth lights. Cool white fluorescents do perfectly well. Position them 6 to 12 inches above the fronds, and buy a simple timer, which should be set to give the plants about fourteen hours of light each day.

temperature

In general, ferns do best with temperatures slightly on the cool side, between 60 and 70° F. Higher temperatures may stimulate the plant's growth, but may also encourage disease. Also, high temperatures throw off the humidity balance; you will have to create more moisture in the air to achieve a respectably high relative humidity. With lower temperatures, you can supply the essential high humidity more easily. Don't push this too far, though. You will be surprised to find that tender ferns can tolerate temperatures

147

down to 40° without being damaged, but you pay a price in considerably slowed growth. At the New York Botanical Garden we have nursed our ferns through several such periods, when accidental heat losses have caused temperatures to drop to something like 40°. Rarely has anything been lost. Some plants have suffered setbacks that slowed their growth for a while, but they have always recovered.

watering

How much? How often? It's not only fern growers who find this one of the trickiest indoor-gardening problems. Killing with kindness by overwatering is probably the most often-committed sin among plant owners. Be advised: there is no such thing as an infallible, all-purpose rule. Your particular needs are controlled by the plant itself, by the soil, the container, the humidity, the light, and so on. It's your responsibility to water the plant when it needs it—and to learn when that is. Two or three times a week is a good way to start for most ferns. Water thoroughly. Don't sprinkle the surface with a few drops and run off to catch your train. The water should go all the way through the soil and even collect in the saucer below, if there is one. However, excess water that does collect there should be thrown out at once. Never let a fern sit in water.

Demise from underwatering is obvious and dramatic. In some cases, as we have seen, the plant goes limp. But far more typically the leaves dry and curl, the crosiers turn brown, and the crown shrivels. Start rescue procedures at once. Soak the whole thing, pot and all, in plenty of water for a considerable time. You'll see some improvement. Leaves that have gone truly dry probably won't recover, but it pays to wait a few days before cutting them off, just in case they do revive. Even if they are lost for good, new leaves will replace them and all will be well, as long as you mend your neglectful ways.

Death from overwatering comes more slowly and is much harder to diagnose. If the soil remains soggy to the touch, you're almost certainly overwatering. Also, watch for poor growth progress. Crosiers don't develop at all in a drowning plant. The leaves remain green, but turn unhealthily dark. Growth ceases. Too much water is forcing all the oxygen out of the soil, causing the roots to rot. Fungi attack them and they cannot perform their function of drawing up nutrients. The plant is headed for a watery grave unless you read the warning signals in time. If you do, you may be able to avert the sad end by repotting in looser, better-draining soil and—of course!—cutting down on watering.

Try to memorize good watering techniques so that you apply them automatically. For one thing, have the water at close to room temperature. For another, don't fling it by bucketfuls over the plants. Use a fine spray or a gentle stream. Water the soil, not the leaves. If sunlight hits the water on a leaf, it turns it into a sort of lens that may burn the leaf; also, such hot moist conditions are exactly the ones in which disease germs multiply most readily.

Finally, treat each plant as an individual. Even when you have six bird's-nests standing in a row, don't assume they'll all be drinking the same amount or at the same rate. Study each one to determine its particular needs. To make my own schedules a bit easier, I usually single out the plants that appear to be drying out most quickly and replant them in heavier soil mixes, which will hold water longer. This makes it more likely that I can work out a schedule by which all my plants can be watered at once.

149

fertilizing

During the spring and summer, ferns like a little additional feeding. Any good nursery offers a selection of house-plant fertilizers and almost all can be used with ferns, provided they are *diluted to half the regular strength* and added to the watering once every three or four weeks. Powdered chemical fertilizer is quite satisfactory, but liquid fish emulsion—if you can put up with the smell—is probably more effective. If you add small amounts of bone meal now and then you'll give progress a noticeable boost. Important: be sure you know when your plant is in a growing, and when in a nongrowing, period, and never fertilize when it's dormant. Feeding it then encourages it to grow when conditions are less than ideal and will make it weaker.

a touch of class

Good basic treatment keeps your plants alive, but even if they flourish you don't want them to be a rough, rambling collection, just growing every which way as if they were still back home in the woods. Since they're indoor plants, you'll want them to show their colors, lines, and overall forms to best advantage. Be prepared to do a bit of trimming and grooming from time to time.

If you're housing *Davallia*, *Humata*, or *Polypodium*, you'll find that the old fronds fall off on their own and cleanly from the rhizome, which cuts your barbering chores down to zero. But with most other ferns the dead fronds tend to hang on until they finally rot off, an unsightly mess that you don't have to put up with. Use a sharp knife or scissors to sever the redundant frond near the base, but not so close that you scrape the rhizome. When an individual leaflet goes brown, cut it off without a qualm. No harm will be done. In fact, you can do this even with part of a leaf—if a tip or edge turns brown, cut off the offending bit and the rest of your leaf will go cheerfully along as if nothing had happened.

It occasionally happens that insecticides, or just ordinary dirt, will spot or dull a leaf's surface. Sponge it with a small amount of detergent in water and rinse well to restore a lively luster. You might use one of the available leaf waxes to heighten the shine, but a healthy plant really needs no help from cosmetics. For myself, I much prefer the natural look and texture of the fronds.

pest control

Ferns in the wild are quite resistant to insect invasion, but unhappily when they move indoors they become as vulnerable as other house plants. Scale insects in particular, if they're in the neighborhood, seem to greet their coming with glad war cries and a swift massing to attack, and unfortunately there are several kinds of scale insects. These small, shell-like creatures attach themselves to a leaf and suck the plant's juices until it is weakened and finally killed. They can be controlled, but it takes strategy and the proper timing. In their juvenile stages, scale insects are mobile and will travel from plant to plant. Obviously it would be best to cut them off at the pass, but you can't because they're too small at this stage to be noticeable. Once they've settled on a particular plant, they lose their legs, form a hard, domed shell, and increase in size until we can finally—and with luck not too late—see and destroy them.

Be especially vigilant about scale if you have *Pellaeas*, *Polystichums*, or *Platyceriums*. These are most often hit, though the insects are quite willing to gorge themselves on

151

almost any kind of fern sooner or later.

You are not helpless in the face of pests. There are several good cures. I use a powdered house-plant insecticide, soluble in water, that contains malathion or sevin. You may have heard that these ingredients can harm ferns, but this is true only of insecticides that come in liquid emulsion form—the oil in the emulsion can be damaging. By using a water-soluble powder, you avoid the danger. Mixed to *half* the recommended dosage and applied either as a spray or by dousing, this treatment controls scale very effectively. Don't stop at one dose. To kill all stages of the infestation, you must repeat the treatment *every* ten days to two weeks until you are certain the enemy has been routed.

Another effective spray is Orthene. There is also Meta-Systox-R, a systemic poison that must be added to the soil either in granular form or as a drench. This is a bit more trouble to use but gives longer-lasting protection.

Whichever insecticide you employ against scale, be particularly careful if you're using it on maidenhairs. These are exceptionally tender, and even the diluted dosage suggested above should be further diluted for them. Some people prefer to pick the insects off by hand rather than spray a maidenhair at all, and if the infestation is really severe the plant probably should be destroyed before it has a chance to infect other plants.

Aphids are another fern enemy. These minute beasts also suck at the plant's tender young parts, especially the tips of young fronds or crosiers. They can rampage over a plant in prodigious numbers. I have seen a crosier so covered by them that it looked black. But they can occasionally be more difficult to spot, and in a casual glance under a frond you might mistake them for sori—which is why you should always do your looking with a hand lens. If what you're looking at moves around, it's not sporangia! Fortunately, you can use the same controls against aphids as against scale. They are also effective against mealybugs, small, flat, white insects that do not move around while you watch them. The hand lens, again, makes these easier to spot.

Whitefly is a nastier problem, since the poisons already discussed don't trouble it a bit. There are a few prepared especially for it, including SBP-1382, which kills the adult insects, and Enstar, which keeps the eggs from developing.

Red spider mites, which live on the leaf underside and cause a yellowish speckling, often accompany too-low humidity. Raising the humidity and spraying with Kelthane should help. Daily misting might be of some use, but if the room is dry the effects are short-lived, and it makes you a slave to the plants. Don't rely on it.

Snails and slugs do great damage by chewing holes in fronds or cutting off young crosiers, thus destroying whole leaves in a few bites. Since they feed mostly at night you won't have much luck picking them off. You may want to try one of the natural traps used to keep their numbers down. Some people claim to have had success in luring slugs away from their plants with grapefruit skins or saucers of beer, which can be discarded once they have trapped the pests. For more certain results use Slugget, either as a spray or a soil drench. Make sure all possible hiding places are treated, including the areas around the plants, such as benches. Spray the undersides of pots, too.

Algae and mosses, which grow quickly on pots and soil, don't do any serious damage, but you may think them unsightly. Since they exist in all except sterilized water, you can never be completely free of them, but if you wash the pots with dilute bleach before planting and use only sterilized soil, you'll reduce the problem.

To repeat: keep a close check for pest problems, because ferns are far from immune. If you see danger, begin control measures at once and repeat the treatment until you are sure you have destroyed generations not killed by the first application.

selecting a plant

Rule One: Remember everything you've learned about the plant's original environment, and then survey your own to see if the plant will be able to get along in the conditions you can provide. Go for those you're sure of because you've had them before, or because you've seen them doing well in similar surroundings. Double-check with the nursery owner if you're buying the plant in a greenhouse. Nursery plants, exposed to high humidity, will look marvelous, but get a professional opinion about their chances with you.

Rule Two: Even when you've made a careful, sensible, realistic choice, there is always some shock involved when a plant is shifted to a new home. Before moving it, cover it with a plastic bag, and after you've established it in place remove the bag only by stages. The simplest technique is to open a small hole in the plastic, then enlarge it a bit each day until you feel the plant has made its adjustment.

If you're not too impatient, select an immature plant. A sporeling that has barely poked its head up into the world is likely to succumb quickly to the stress of a new environment, while a full-grown plant, set in its ways, will also have a hard time adapting to your conditions. Something in between is what you want. Look for new growth: new crosiers, healthy leaves, a good growing tip.

No matter how good a nursery you're buying from, take time for a good close insect examination before you decide. If you see nothing to arouse your suspicion, fine—but even then it's wise to isolate the newcomer in your home for a few days so you can watch it. In fact, it does no harm to give it a gentle treatment with insecticide just in case; it's good insurance.

ferns that come in from the wild

If you're interested in this aspect of fern growing, the first discovery you'll make is that you've wandered into a contentious hornet's nest. We don't know all that much about what will or won't succeed. The experts disagree. You're free to try anything.

For example, if you live in a temperate climate you'll very likely be told that your local wild ferns won't make it indoors because they have to have a winter cold experience. But the evidence is far from positive, and many experts question it. Probably once again the key is humidity. If you can boost yours as described earlier, and you stumble over a plant you're eager to try, do it. Certainly the smaller ones—the fragile, the walking, the several spleenworts—can be used in your terrariums. I've seen plenty of the larger ones going along at a great rate in greenhouses—*Dryopteris, Polystichum, Woodwardia*—but some do seem to get tired if not given a winter rest. If someone tries to discourage you, remind him that the Japanese and Tsus-sima holly ferns, and also the felt fern, are natives of cool temperate regions, and they've been taken for granted as temperate-area indoor plants for a long time.

Some of the fern allies are easily acclimated and can be

paricularly effective indoors. The shining clubmoss (*Lyco-podium lucidulum*), which does not have the fungi in its roots that make nutrition a problem with many other club-mosses, can even be grown outside of a terrarium or other humidity trap. I've had some shining clubmoss growing in a bonsai dish on my office desk for more than a year. I have only to remember to keep the soil moist, and it flourishes. In fact, it crowded out its neighbor, a dwarf scouring rush (*Equisetum scirpoides*). This one and its relative *E. varie-gatum* remain less than 8 inches tall and display a distinctive texture and form that make them excellent house plants.

Let me repeat what I said at the start of this chapter: our experience with indoor ferns has so far been confined to relatively few species. We know there must be many ex-cellent possibilities out there that simply haven't been worked with yet. For example, the enormous genus *Ela-phoglossum*, with more than five hundred species with un-divided fronds, shows great diversity in its hairs and scales, an attraction that could make many of its members desirable house plants. Some are smooth, some are sprinkled with black hairs, some are margined with golden scales. They range from dark green through bluish-green to yellow-green. Their sizes vary. Yet as of now only a couple have been looked at for horticultural possibilities.

Genera that we already know will grow well—*Humata*, *Pyrrosia*, and *Asplenium*, for example—are ready to supply many additional species for growers willing to experiment with them. Recently I brought into our New York Botanical Garden greenhouses a specimen of *Asplenium exiguum*, an interesting spleenwort from Mexico. On its native turf it is once-divided and grows 3 to 6 inches tall. In the high humidity of our cloud chamber it developed young plants at the ends of each pinna, making a necklace of babies around each leaf. When I examined dried specimens of the original plants from the wild, I realized that I had not stumbled on a mutation. The buds are always there encircling the leaves, but since the plants grow in relatively dry mountains, they don't enjoy the humidity that would help them develop into plantlets. In our high-humidity conditions, or in any closed container—bottle garden, terrarium—they thrive and develop new plants in great profusion.

The possibilities are not unlimited. Humidity is not the only factor that determines what will or will not succeed. In some cases, for example, we will surely run into the fungus problem we already know about in the roots of the clubmosses. But even in such cases, if we bring the plant in for study and determine that there is a fungus essential to its culture, we could probably introduce it into the soil and develop for ourselves still another attractive domesticated fern. There may be other problems: missing minerals, perhaps, or other nutrients. The point is that fern culture is far from an oversophisticated horticultural activity. Everyone who is attracted by ferns and interested in them stands a good chance of making a contribution to our too-slim body of knowledge. Plants need to be brought in, experimented with under home conditions, and finally reproduced by commercial nurseries. The American Fern Society can tell you about the research already being done, and what possible part you might play in it.

outdoor cultivation

ferns in the outdoor garden are no problem. The range of possibilities is large, and if you make the right choices, your plants will have little trouble settling in. For a foolproof start, investigate the ferns that grow spontaneously in your area. Almost every part of the United States boasts several local native ferns. Since they've already succeeded in the local climate, there's every chance that they can be moved into your garden without going under. But if you're doubtful of your expertise in transplanting them from the wild—and it can be tricky—your local nurseries are sure to have some of the common native ferns on hand.

There's almost no limit to the candidates if you live in a warm area. More ferns are native to warm climates than to cold, so at once your choices expand. Further, the multitudinous tropical species can usually adjust to temperatures slightly cooler than those they've grown up in. What they can't stand, and can never be trained to stand, is the damaging cold of true northern winters. When a tropical fern is moved to, say, Florida or southern California, it can be given additional water to make up for the occasional dry seasons it will encounter. It can be protected from strong direct sun and wind by high walls, well-placed shade trees, or specially constructed lathe houses. Given this kind of help, many tropical ferns flourish in semitropical and even warm temperate climates. But there is little defense against cold weather, and it does limit your options.

ferns for your environment

As a general rule, if you live in a warm climate you should be able to grow out-of-doors almost any fern that will grow in a greenhouse. These include such spectacular plants as the tall, stately tree ferns and the fleshy *Angiopteris evecta* with its 9-foot fronds. You can create lush, dramatic effects. Tropical ferns can be naturalized in a wooded area, or, with the right kind of protection from a lathe house or other sun- and wind-screening device, they can be developed into simulated rain forests. A lathe house is a worthwhile investment. With the environmental controls it provides, you can let your creativity fly. You can add some epiphytes to your mini-forest, attached to trees. Terrestrial ferns can be introduced below as ground cover. Besides protecting plants, lathe houses offer support for staghorn arrangements and all kinds of hanging baskets.

Moving north from warm regions, your possibilities grow gradually more limited as the threat of freezing temperatures increases. But there is a wide gray area intermediate between the absolutely hardy and the absolutely tender plants. Some tropical ferns can survive a light frost. Some may be hardy, or marginally hardy, a considerable distance away from the tropics. This is another research area in which surprisingly little has been done, and in many cases the only way to find out for sure what will work in your area is to do your own experimenting. Take a chance with some fern that appeals to you—providing you don't live at the northernmost tip of Minnesota. See if you can coax it into accepting what your garden has to offer.

However, coming up to the cooler temperate areas, we have to face the fact that the only sensible fern choices you can make must be from among those that can withstand seasonal below-freezing temperatures. Actually, there's a pretty good selection. There are more than a hundred species native to the northeastern United States. To be honest,

161

162

Lady fern (*Athyrium filix-femina*).

many of these are rare, and some require very special conditions, but after all the putting and taking is done there remain at least thirty species frequent and likely enough to be easily obtained.

The Christmas fern (*Polystichum acrostichoides*), one of the most common, has attractive leathery evergreen fronds. The lady fern (*Athyrium filix-femina*) is so common that the sporelings often form a carpet in moist, shaded lawn areas. It grows vigorously and is easily transplanted. The shield or buckler ferns (*Dryopteris*) are also good growers and will give you interesting color in shades of dark green, yellow-green, and bluish-green. The plumelike fronds and vase-

Northern maidenhair (*Adiantum pedatum*).

163

shaped crown of the ostrich fern (*Matteuccia struthiopteris*) are decorative, and it is widely planted in temperate regions. A favorite group both indoors and out is the maidenhairs, with their fine, delicate leaflets on slender, wiry black stalks. Although most species of this family are tropical, there are some, such as *Adiantum pedatum* and *A. venustum*, that can withstand cold winters.

While I would always suggest starting with local specimens, there's no need to limit yourself to these forever if you're in a temperate zone. After a time you might look around (in nurseries, naturally, unless you're planning to mount a botanical expedition) for some of the many species from other temperate regions of the world.

The western sword fern (*Polystichum munitum*) and the giant chain fern (*Woodwardia fimbriata*) of northwestern North America are handsome 4-foot-high plants with large, bristly margined, deep green fronds. They make an attractive display either singly or, as they are often used, in groups.

The Japanese painted fern (*Athyrium niponicum* cv. *Pictum*) is one of the most popular Asian ferns to have come into western temperate gardens. Its coloration is striking: each leaflet has a wine-red center bordered by gray-green margins. It dies down each autumn, but rebounds every spring and spreads well. Another Japanese favorite, the autumn fern (*Dryopteris erythrosora*), also displays attractive color. The young fronds have an unusual reddish cast and the sori are bright pink.

Some of the most fascinating of hardy ferns are the English crested ferns. Toward the end of the nineteenth century the English, in the grip of the fern fever we talked about in Chapter 6, scoured the countryside for variations of their

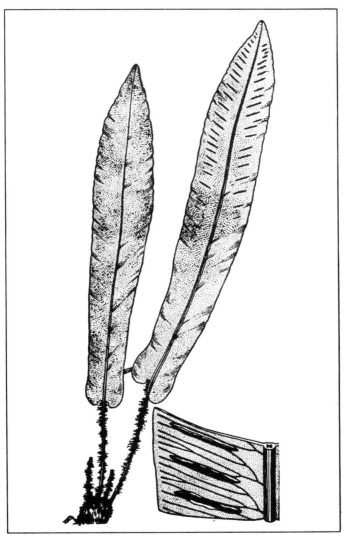

Hart's-tongue (*Phyllitis scolopendrium*).

165

native ferns and came up with a staggering number—over a thousand. There were three hundred sixty varieties of the soft shield fern (*Polystichum setiferum*), three hundred of the lady fern, and hundreds of the male fern (*Dryopteris filix-mas*) and the hart's-tongue (*Phyllitis scolopendrium*). The variations were in the degree of cutting, the size of the frond, the ruffling of frond margins, and the forking at the tips of frond and leaflet. In his magnificent book *Hardy Ferns* (London, Faber & Faber, 1968), nurseryman Reginald Kaye estimates that perhaps 60 percent of the old English varieties have been lost over the years, largely through lack of care during the two world wars. Most modern gardeners, he says, are now totally unaware of them. Fortunately, the dedicated English are still growing quite a number of varieties, but that has not made them widely available in other parts of the world. In other words, we're making do with fewer varieties of ferns than we might have had if we'd taken the right kind of care of them.

However, some of the lost varieties may well be rediscovered in nature or among the offspring of ferns grown from spores. There is always the possibility that new varieties may appear—new or recurring mutations, even recombinations of characteristics that can add up to a different appearance. Look among sporelings, both in nature and in your own back yard, so to speak, for unusual plants.

While we may bemoan the "lost" ferns, we're still left with plenty of possibilities for temperate-zone outdoor use. Reginald Kaye lists several from outside England; Mr. Johannes Hovland of Øystese, Norway, grows three hundred species and varieties from around the world in his fern garden, which is obviously in the northern range of temperate. And exciting developments are soon to come from the New

York Botanical Garden, which is working with members of the American Fern Society to learn which other ferns are out there in the rest of the world that might survive well in our temperate environment. The program, which will go a long way toward filling our research gap, is being conducted at the Cary Arboretum, about seventy miles north of New York City, where the Botanical Garden has established a Fern Glen in which it is testing the hardiness of as many species from other temperate zones of the world as it can obtain, together with most of our own native ferns. Previously unresearched plants from the Pacific Northwest, Japan, and northern Europe, as well as many from the Himalayas, New Zealand, and high-elevation tropical America are being studied. Surprising discoveries have already been made. The Mexican *Dryopteris pseudo-filix-mas*, for example, has proved to be hardy in this latitude, considerably north of its native terrain. Several of our own southern ferns have made the move without much trauma. Two *Dryopteris* species from hot, damp Louisiana, *D. ludoviciana* and *D. australis*, are making it through northern winters without special protection. Why they do not migrate north on their own is an interesting question, and one that no one has yet been able to answer.

It turns out also that some ferns we've been careful to shelter as house plants are quite hardy outdoors. The Japanese holly fern (*Cyrtomium falcatum*) and the closely related *C. fortunei* and *C. caryotideum*, as well as the Tsussima holly fern (*Polystichum tsus-simense*), have a place in the outdoor garden as well as on your window sill. The Japanese climbing fern (*Lygodium japonicum*) is marginally hardy as far north as Connecticut. Within a couple of years, spores of hundreds of possible species will have been grown

167

and tested outdoors at the Cary Arboretum Fern Glen, and we will know a great deal more about the cold tolerance of plants we have heretofore written off for our north-temperate gardens.

creating the garden

Shade, soil, moisture. Keep these factors in mind when you set out to establish an outdoor fern garden. Once again, though, don't be taken in by the myth about ferns needing deep shade. I've seen it written under impressive auspices that if a corner of your property is so dark nothing will grow there, it's made to order for ferns. Not so; don't try it. True, they need protection from the scorching midday sun and stiff, drying winds, but they also need light if they're to grow well.

What suits them best is partial or mixed shade, with a few hours of sunlight each day—*not* through the midday hours—or a position where they're exposed to the open sky on the north side of a house, between buildings, or in window wells. If you're lucky enough to have a wooded area, you can set them within it in a place where patches of sunlight will touch them at some time during the day. Or you can place them at the border of your woods, where foliage will shade them for part of the day. When you go exploring for local ferns, observe how they have placed themselves: they'll be flourishing in light woods or at the edges of clearings. In deeply shaded woods there are no ferns at all. Take your cues from this as you survey your own land for the right spot.

Having found a place with the right shade-and-light combination, consider the soil. Happily, outdoor ferns are not fussy about soil. They like it a touch on the acid side, with moderate drainage, and they can't stand it to become bone dry—which means that you can establish them in almost any kind of soil, because most soil, with a little doctoring, can be brought to this balance. My own fern garden started out in the most plebeian of media—pure sand fill, of which there happened to be quite a lot beside my house. This would have been too free-draining, so I began by adding about 2 inches of compost over the entire area, slowly working it into the soil. The ferns were planted with extra compost in each hole, and wood chips were strewn over the surface to help conserve moisture. I've added more compost each year, and after only two or three years the soil became as rich aś you could wish. A small amount of bone meal once or twice a year is also helpful.

If I had had only heavy clay soil available, I would, of course, have treated it differently. Clay does not allow enough oxygen to get through to the roots, and they suffer. I would have added organic matter and a good deal of sand to loosen the clay and provide better drainage.

A special note about compost: beware of adding undecomposed matter to the soil, such as raw compost, grass clippings, sawdust, and the like. If this "green manure" is worked into the soil around the plants, it will rob them of nitrogen as it itself decays. Always allow material like this to decompose before you use it, or else apply it only as a mulch on the soil surface.

Once the soil is prepared, you're ready to plant. Incidentally, don't make the common mistake of leaving bare-rooted plants around unprotected while you're solving your other problems. The roots will dry out, and if the plants survive at all, they will have two strikes against them from the start. When you are digging up a plant yourself, get it

169

out with as much soil around it as you can. The roots should be well protected with dirt until you replant, and they should be disturbed as little as possible. Great disturbance shocks the plant and reduces its capacity to draw water from the soil until it can produce new rootlets to do the job. If the plant comes to you bare-rooted, or nearly so, tie a plastic bag around the roots, or at least pad them round with moist rags or newspapers.

It's also a good idea to prepare the plant by cutting off any broken fronds. If it has a good root ball, you can stop trimming at this point. Otherwise, it's best to cut off about one-third of the total fronds to minimize water loss from the leaf surfaces. If you've kept a sizable root ball, and will be sure to provide plenty of water as the fern gets established in its new situation, you can sometimes take a chance on retaining all the plant's good leaves. This has to be left to your judgment and experience.

As with any garden, you'll save trouble and get your best results by planning it in advance. In your mind or on paper, decide exactly how you want the plants placed. You might even lay them in position for a dry run. Only when you are sure of where everything will go are you ready to dig. The hole for each plant should be somewhat larger than its root ball. Before the plant goes in, add peat or compost to the hole, and water it to start the roots off with plenty of moisture. Then note the habit of the rhizome—whether ascending or creeping horizontally—and orient it in the same way as it goes into its new home.

It's very important to plant the fern at the same level at which it previously grew, and equally important that the growing tip remain uncovered, slightly above the soil. Tamp soil around the root ball to firm it in place, but be careful not to disturb the angle you've decided is the correct one. Add compost as a top dressing and mulch.

You'll run into a special problem with ferns that have slender, long-creeping rhizomes and so cannot easily be held on the surface of the soil. The best technique is to make a shallow trench in which to lay the rhizome and then sprinkle it over lightly with soil. Ferns like these should be planted no more than half an inch deep.

When planting is complete, give everything a good long drink. If you feel like adding a little something extra, surround the plants with wood chips. They'll help to keep moisture in the soil and discourage weeds.

And now for the good news. You're practically finished. If you've done everything correctly up to this point, your fern garden will need very little maintenance. For the first few weeks water liberally and frequently to assure early growth. After those first weeks, rainfall should take care of the watering requirements—except, of course, in times of drought, when you'll need to be on hand with your garden hose.

In the spring, you must snap to attention. The fern garden should be cleaned and made ready before the crosiers start to unfurl, because they are very fragile and crisp and as they begin to enlarge will break off easily at a slight touch. Remove all weeds, branches, and leaves by hand. Never use a hoe or a rake, as they could damage the shallow root systems or break off the fiddleheads. This is a good time to add some well-rotted compost or mulch to the soil.

In the autumn, before the leaves fall, supply another helping of compost or mulch, and when the leaves do come down let them lie on the fern garden as additional mulch. They act as insulation over the winter, and later break down

171

to improve the soil's nutrients and texture. In late fall, start protecting the ferns that are marginally hardy for your area, and any you suspect of being so. You can do this by placing leaves and branches over the plants, or more elaborately by setting open-topped boxes covered with coarse screening over the plants. These provide some insulation and help prevent frost heaving in late winter and early spring.

Ferns grown from spores can be placed outside the first year, but they must be protected. For the first winter, and usually the second as well, they should be sheltered in a cold frame. In their third year out-of-doors they can be gradually weaned to the full brunt of winter.

Some of the more aggressive ferns need to be kept in check by occasional thinning. The prolific stolons of the ostrich fern, the wide-creeping rhizomes of the sensitive fern (*Onoclea sensibilis*), the New York fern (*Thelypteris noveboracensis*), and sometimes the lady fern will try to take everything over if you don't thin them back to their allotted space. Other species, while not especially aggressive, may produce offshoots where you don't want them, but these can easily be removed for planting elsewhere. In the case of crown-forming plants the young plants should be removed, because they detract from the appearance of the large crown and even, with time, displace it. The crown-formers *Polystichum* and *Dryopteris* may produce young plants from the sides of the stems. When they are large enough to have their own roots—perhaps one-fourth the size of the parent—these can be removed with a sharp knife. Cut close to the main stem, but not so close as to damage it. Widely branching rhizomes can be divided easily: cut through them with a sharp knife or trowel, or break off by hand a section along the edge of the colony.

special effects

You can group your ferns together in a fern garden if you prefer them that way, but if you'd rather mix things up a bit there's no reason they can't mingle with the rest of your garden. You can landscape most attractively with ferns as long as you match fern and environment with care and don't neglect the plants' broad light-and-sun needs. Try to simulate, or at least approximate, their natural habitats.

For example, if you have a wet, even swampy, area, there are several swamp-loving ferns that will take to it and feel as if they've never left home. Try the cinnamon (*Osmunda cinnamomea*), the royal (*O. regalis*), the ostrich, the marsh (*Thelypteris palustris*), and the chain ferns (*Wood-*

Fragile fern (*Cystopteris fragilis*).

174

Common polypody (*Polypodium virginianum*).

Top: Walking fern
(*Camptosorus rhizophyllus*). Bottom: Maidenhair
spleenwort (*Asplenium trichomanes*).

wardia areolata and *W. virginica*). If you have a pond or pool that gets strong sunlight, try the water clover (*Marsilea*), which has four leaflets that float on the water or rise slightly above it.

There are a number of ferns that do well on the ledges or in the crevices of a rock wall. It's not difficult to create such an environment (see pages 184–85, "Building a Cobble"), but if you've already got one, you can go right to work with the *Woodsias*, the delicate fragile fern (*Cystopteris fragilis*), and its relative the bulblet bladder-fern (*C. bulbifera*). Despite its heavy-handed name, the bladder-fern boasts slender, gracefully arching fronds plus the additional asset of producing tiny budlike bulbils, which fall off readily and root themselves in moist soil, producing rich growth. It needs a site with plenty of moisture. The *Aspleniums* are mostly rock ferns, and several, like the ebony and the maidenhair, grow well in cultivation.

Some of the polypodies (*Polypodium*) are rock ferns, and the hart's-tongue too will display its glossy green straps against rocks with interesting effect. In the neighborhood of limestone rocks, you can rely on the cliff-brake (*Pellaea*) and the walking fern (*Camptosorus rhizophyllus*), as well as on some of the spleenworts and the maidenhairs. (Wherever you have these lime-loving plants, it's a good idea to sprinkle marble chips around them for the lime they'll add to the soil.)

Except for the cliff-brake, all the above-mentioned ferns need a good amount of moisture along with their rocks. In drier areas of your rock wall, besides the *Pellaeas*, try the lip fern (*Cheilanthes*), the cloak fern (*Notholaena*), and the silverback (*Pityrogramma*) if you are in a warm, dry area.

Rocks also work well with some of the very small fern

species. You can take advantage of the parsley fern (*Cryptogramma crispa*), the walking fern, the wall rue (*Asplenium ruta-muraria*), species of *Ceterach*, and *Blechnum penna-marina*. There are also miniature varieties of some larger species: *Adiantum pedatum* var. *minor*, *Polystichum setiferum* var. *congestum*, and *Athyrium filix-femina* var. *minutissimum*.

Ferns that do well in the open areas of your garden come with a warning attached: watch out for takeover spreading

The parsley fern is only about 8 inches tall.

tactics. Two of the best for open areas are the hay-scented fern and the sensitive fern, but both must be curbed by pruning if you don't plan to turn your garden over to them. The hay-scented (*Dennstaedtia punctilobula*) is so rampant that it rarely appears on lists of protected species, as most North American ferns do, but so far I haven't found it a problem. It does indeed spread rapidly, but on the other hand it enjoys sun, and its fluffy yellow-green fronds soften the harsh outlines of any exposed rocks, bringing them into

178

The deer fern
(*Blechnum spicant*) has an evergreen
rosette of dark green leaves.

Ferns often make a fine
border to a garden. Here the Japanese
painted fern and the northern maidenhair
line a wood-chip path.

179

the general landscape. It does a good job of filling in areas that might otherwise be difficult to manage. The sensitive fern appears in nature in wet meadows and swamps, but it does well in shaded areas, spreads quickly, and yet can be kept within bounds by occasional pruning.

You may never have considered ferns for foundation plantings, or to edge a patio, but there are some that can be used very effectively. Large *Dryopteris* species can be combined here with the small, pale green oak fern (*Gymnocarpium dryopteris*) or the colorful Japanese painted fern. The large vase-shaped ostrich fern works well with smaller species of different textures, such as the maidenhair. The Christmas fern, with its more spreading fronds, makes a low mass that can be an attractive border on its own. If you're looking for a border to a walkway, the maidenhair and the Japanese painted fern are especially good, since they are low, delicate, and colorful, while at the same time hardy and fast-spreading. Even the large, coarse, unruly bracken can be pressed into service as a border plant if the space is open enough so that it will not be out of proportion. But you must confine bracken to its allotted space by sinking a stiff edging strip of metal or plastic into the ground, to limit the spread of the subterranean rhizome as it reaches outward.

Consider, also, the ferns you can use for color, many of them evergreen and vivid throughout the winter: species of the wood ferns, holly ferns, polypodies, spleenworts, hart's-tongues, walking ferns. The fertile fronds of the sensitive and ostrich ferns stand as sentinels through the snow, ready at the first touch of spring to release their spores. In spring and summer too ferns give you the advantage, unique to this plant group, of the color in their unrolling fiddleheads.

Some are quite showy; all are noticeable. In North America the most conspicuous of all is the one up earliest in the spring—the cinnamon fern. Its clusters of young crosiers arising in the swamps and wet ditches in late April stand with their heads huddled toward a center, like conspirators discussing their spring strategy. They bear dense white hairs that turn cinnamon-colored as the fronds mature.

From the royal fern and the maidenhairs you will get beautiful pink crosiers. This color is inconspicuous on the forest floor, where it blends with the brown leaves, but it will be a clear and lovely springtime asset in your garden. And if your patio is bordered with Christmas fern, the spring fiddleheads, densely clothed with white, chaffy scales, will give you an unexpectedly interesting edging.

Look also for fall color. There isn't a great deal of it, and most of it is in shades of gold and yellow, but it is still attractive. The *Osmundas* and the hay-scented fern turn as bright a yellow as do many trees.

When you think about mixing ferns with other plants, remember that it's not only green plants they complement. Many flowering plants combine well with them. Native plants like wild geranium, campanula, columbine, hepatica, bloodroot, and violet all provide excellent touches of color and variation in texture. Jack-in-the-pulpit is especially good, raising its handsome three-lobed leaves and hooded inflorescence above many of the smaller ferns, then adding bright late-summer color with its orange fruits. Solomon seal, foam flower, and bishop's cap add touches of white or pink without becoming garish. You can also mix flowers with ferns in such a way that they will keep things interesting in early spring before the ferns are fully up and about. Azaleas make a brilliant background for unrolling fiddle-

181

182

The cinnamon fern bears
its spores on special slender fronds
in the center of the crown.

Ferns can be used in a
garden by themselves or mixed
with flowering plants.

heads. Spring flowering bulbs—daffodils, tulips, crocuses—act as heralds of the more abundant show to come. By the time the bulbs are finished, the ferns are up, hiding the fading leaves of the earlier plants. I have also mixed the white and pink plumes of astilbes with ferns. A border of primulas is effective around ferns during the summer, and through late summer and fall the pink flowers and red-bottomed leaves of the hardy begonia are vivid against fern greens. Colorful foliage plants are also good partners: I like both the variegated hostas, with their stripes of green and yellow or white, and the pale green-and-white leaves of snow-on-the-mountain.

Another way to use ferns is to naturalize them in a section of woodland, if you have one. In such settings it's a good and natural idea to start by creating paths of wood chips, which you can often get free from town highway departments. These give you the rough shape of a plan; log steps and split-log benches are not difficult to add and give the right visual blend to the area, where you want nothing showy or contrived-looking. One caution, however: examine your woodland before you invest your time. If no ferns grow there spontaneously, there's probably good reason for the lack—poor soil, perhaps, or too much shade or not enough moisture. Not all woodlands are ideal for ferns, and while with a lot of effort you might be able to alter the conditions, it's wise to think twice before you try. Instead of taking on a battle you have small chance of winning, you might do better to find another, more promising spot.

building a cobble

If you already have a rock wall, congratulations—and not only because it combines so well with ferns! If you don't have one, don't despair. It's not very difficult to build yourself a modest one, the kind called a cobble. Of course, if you're up to building a formal rock wall many yards long and several feet high, don't let these words stop you. But even a few rocks placed together in some sort of order can become a highly effective setting for your ferns.

Start by choosing a site in open shade, preferably where there is good moisture in the ground. If you can find such a place that also offers a slope into which you can build the rockwork, excellent: freestanding rockwork does not fit as naturally into its surroundings. For your stones, try to get sandstone or limestone—weathered, not freshly cut. If you can pilfer from an old rock wall, so much the better.

Before the rocks go down, prepare the site. Dig into the soil a foot or so, and lay down some good fern soil. Then add fern soil behind the rocks as you put them in. There are two ways to incorporate the ferns in the cobble: you can leave pockets between the rocks into which the ferns go later, or you can keep the rocks close-fitted, in which case you put the ferns in with them as you go along. Pack soil and compost into the pockets along with the fern. You can even wrap the fern's roots in moss for added moisture-holding capacity. Since the rocks are basically rather dry because they drain rapidly, you need to incorporate as many moisture-retaining elements as you can. If possible, add to the moisture potential in other ways: keep the wall in the shade; don't make it too tall; add organic material in every possible crevice. If you've been able to build into the side of a slope the rocks will be backed with earth, improving the moisture. If you're concerned about dryness, you may even want to run a dry well nearby to add to the general soil moisture.

185

haunts and habitats

f you just want a fern or two around the place, you can always go to a nursery, point one out, and ask, "Will that grow in my living room (or garden)?" If the nursery owner says yes, you take it away. It's the simplest way. You're bounded by the nursery owner's knowledge, and certainly your choices are limited, but it doesn't take much effort. If you really want to grow ferns, however, it's far more satisfying to start accumulating information of your own. When you know where and under what conditions ferns grow in the wild, you'll be able to make your own judgments about which ones hold some promise for you, and why certain others will not do well in cultivation at all.

We've already seen that though the fern population is world-wide, the distribution is far from even. Because of the need most species have for good humidity, mixed shade, and moderate to warm temperatures, the highest concentrations are in rain forests or warm temperate regions. There are 150 species in western Europe, 130 in the Soviet Union, 380 in America north of Mexico, and 200 in New Zealand. In contrast, the tiny island of Jamaica has 600 species. Costa Rica and Panama together have 900. Malaya has 500. Obviously, damp warmth is what most ferns want.

Nevertheless, some of them wander. Probably the most widespread of all is the fragile fern, which travels because it is, or has learned to be, adaptable. It is found on nearly every continent in moist temperate forests. It is also found in more tropical regions, but here it takes itself to higher elevations. While exploring southern Mexico, I ventured to the top of Cerro Zempoaltepetl, 11,000 feet high. The only fern growing up there was the fragile fern, nestled shyly

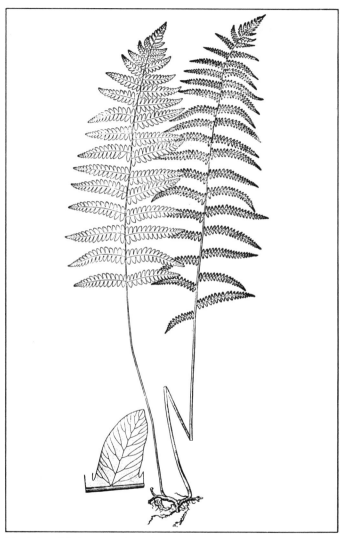

Marsh fern (*Thelypteris palustris*).

189

among the rocks at the base of a sacrificial altar.

Since the fragile fern is always small (usually 4 to 10 inches) and hides as though bashful of attracting attention, its ruggedness comes as a surprise. Other wide-ranging ferns tend to be more noticeable, like the marsh fern, the maidenhair spleenwort, and the running pine (*Lycopodium clavatum*), all of which occur on five or six continents. Most conspicuous of all is the brash and almost uncontrollable bracken, which grows up to 16 feet tall. It occurs everywhere from high mountains to lowland tropics, ready to cover vast areas with its fast-spreading underground rhizomes.

But most ferns have a more restricted distribution. They commonly range along mountain or river systems, either on a single continent or adjacent continents. Many species run from Mexico down the Andes, for example, or from the lowlands of the Amazon basin along the Brazilian coast to Central America and the West Indies.

Some show even more restricted patterns and are found around the world only at a particular latitude. Certain tropical species grow only in tropical parts of America, Asia, and Africa: *Acrostichum aureum* in brackish marshes, *Ceratopteris thalictroides* in wet ditches and slow-moving streams; *Pteris cretica* and *Adiantum capillus-veneris* on masonry and limestone walls; *Dryopteris parallelogramma* on high mountains.

Some of the more temperate species are circumboreal— they grow only across the high northern latitudes of North America, Europe, and Asia. This nearly continuous band of distribution is typical of several species of horsetails and clubmosses, the oak fern, and the grape ferns. The species *Hypolepis rugulosa, Blechnum penna-marina,* and *Todea*

Oak fern (*Gymnocarpium dryopteris*).

192

Anemia phyllitidis.

barbara are circumaustral—they occur in southern South America, New Zealand, and South Africa.

What we realize when we look at distribution patterns is that plants, while they cannot move, can nevertheless migrate. Over the generations, they can extend their ranges. Spores fall to the ground a few feet away from a parent plant, new plants grow up, and their spores in turn travel a short distance farther. In this manner a species will expand its growing range over the years unless and until it encounters an inhibiting situation. This block can occur in a number of ways. The area around it may itself be limited. The fern may not produce enough spores, or it may be surrounded by more aggressive plants with which it cannot compete. One of the basic problems we have yet to unravel is why some ferns spread easily while others don't seem capable of doing so and have a hard time even becoming established.

Some species are found today in patterns that suggest long-range dispersal, but they can also be explained as remnants of ancient continuous distribution. For example, there are ferns common to Mexico and the Himalayas, and others that are found in Japan and the eastern United States. Those in the circumaustral, or southern, band were probably in closer proximity in that early time before the continents separated. The continuous distribution that once existed with some species may have been further interrupted by alterations in world climate that eliminated those species in certain areas, leaving disconnected patches in what appear now to be unrelated parts of the world. We draw some of these inferences from the genus *Anemia,* which is found today largely in tropical America. We have found some of its more primitive species surviving in Africa and southern

India. We know that in Cretaceous times, 150 million years ago, *Anemia* occurred nearly world-wide, since fossil *Anemias* have been found on nearly every continent as far north as Canada, northern Europe, and Siberia. But apparently the subsequent cooling of the earth has greatly changed the range of the contemporary plants, restricting them to warmer regions.

Not only do plants migrate, they don't necessarily take vast stretches of time to do it, nor do they extend their ranges only when triggered by major climatic changes or geologic upheavals. A number of ferns are right now very actively advancing their frontiers. Some are escapees from cultivation. *Pteris vittata,* for example, native to Asia and Africa, now grows freely in the southeastern United States, the West Indies, and some cities in South America. Other species have not been cultivated, but seem to be invading the New World on their own. The genus *Thelypteris* is especially aggressive. Earlier in this century *Thelypteris torresiana* and *T. dentata,* African natives, were entirely restricted to the Old World, but during the past thirty years they have sprung up in widespread parts of America, far from any metropolitan areas. Almost in the same period, an Oriental cousin, *T. opulenta,* has mounted its own invasion on our Pacific side, and now appears on the west coasts of Central and South America.

In some sad cases, a species' reach will exceed its grasp— it will try to expand its range but, being at the limit of its hardiness, will fail. Sometimes such an ambitious plant does manage to establish itself tenuously, but, trying to cope with an environment it cannot adjust to, it soon dies out. This happened with the tropical forking fern *Dicranopteris flexuosa.* Common in the American tropics, it managed to work

Thelypteris dentata has
become a common tropical American
fern in just the last forty years.

its way into three localities of the southern United States, but it has already died out in two of them. *Diplazium lonchophyllum* has established itself in only two places in Louisiana, though it is abundant farther south. The prospects for *Grammitis nimbata* are similar. Spores of this fern were apparently blown by a hurricane from the West Indies to western North Carolina, where it survives in its only North American station.

It's a commonly held belief that ferns are found everywhere except in the most arid deserts and the coldest regions of the world. True, the deserts have yet to surprise us. But there are a few ferns that have shown themselves able to withstand extreme cold—though perhaps there are none

Arctic tundra, northern Alaska. There are ferns and fern allies that have adapted even to this seemingly forbidding habitat.

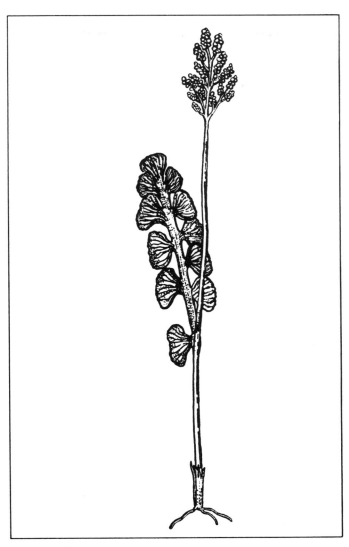

Moonwort (*Botrychium lunaria*).

at the absolute top of the world. The moonwort and the fragile fern—the same family that made it 11,000 feet up that Mexican mountain—go well above the tree line in the North. Several of the horsetails, including the dwarf scouring rush and the variegated scouring rush, survive even farther north, well into the Arctic tundra. By and large, however, the mass of the world's ferns is divided between the temperate and the tropical climatic bands.

temperate deciduous forests

A cool, moist, deep green forest with assorted ferns on the earthy floor is what most of us envision when we think of ferns in the wild. It's a far from unrealistic image. Such temperate woods—in eastern and northwestern North America, in Europe, New Zealand, eastern Australia, Japan, and the higher elevations of tropical areas—are indeed a typical fern habitat, with the high humidity, partial shade, and loose, moist, slightly acid soil that ferns do best in. Many of the temperate ferns will be found there, including the holly ferns (*Polystichum*), wood ferns (*Dryopteris*), and lady ferns (*Athyrium*).

tropical rain forests

Having talked about how ferns proliferate in tropical forests, I must now back off a bit from the generalization. Lowland tropical forests are often poor in ferns. The reasons are solidly environmental, consistent with what we know about ferns' needs. Lowland forests are often fairly dry, or at least have a dry season, they're often too dark, and they're generally too hot—few ferns like very high temperatures.

Still, there are a few groups that do thrive here. You'll find the maidenhairs (*Adiantum*), halberd ferns, climbing

The cool wet forests of Oregon
make an ideal habitat for ferns. Seen
in this photograph is mostly the western
sword fern (*Polystichum munitum*).

ferns, the ubiquitous bracken, and sometimes the genus *Lindsaea,* which resembles the maidenhair so closely that the two are often confused. Much of the lowland forest is cut over, yet the ferns that flourish here are so widespread that most are not in danger of extinction. Uninterrupted by mountains or other barriers, they migrate at will over sometimes large areas. Only a few of the rarer types are threatened. One is the curious dagger fern (*Dictyoxiphium panamense*) of Central America. A close relative of the halberd, it is differentiated by bearing its sori along the margins of the undivided leaves, rather than in round dots on the undersides of divided leaves. It hybridizes with one species of the halberd to form an intermediate species with vari-shaped sori scattered all over the leaf undersides. Unfortunately, the habitats for these plants are rapidly disappearing, and unless it is deliberately preserved, the dagger fern will go, too.

It's when we leave the tropical lowlands and start climbing into medium-elevation forests that we truly hit fern pay dirt. Here—in such regions as the Andes, eastern Mexico, Malaya, New Guinea, Jamaica—ferns can luxuriate in constant rainfall, with year-long high humidity rarely if ever interrupted by a dry spell. When there is a distinct and cyclical dry season, the contrast in vegetation is interesting: we get a good look at it when we compare the Atlantic and Pacific slopes of southern Mexico. Both have wet forests, but on the Pacific side there is an annual dry season several months long, limiting the growth of filmy ferns, tree ferns, and other high-humidity ferns and fern allies. On the Atlantic slopes there is rain or mist every day of every year, permitting a much wider range of pteridophytes to flourish.

Temperate-region ferns are almost all terrestrial; they

stick to the ground because they would dry out rapidly if they tried to grow on the surrounding tree trunks. But in wet tropical forests the tree trunks are fairly covered with mosses, liverworts, and ferns—epiphytes that can live richly on the nutrients and moisture from the bark of the host or from the detritus that collects in branches and crevices. The growing area for ferns is therefore much expanded in these forests, and about two-thirds of the native ferns take advantage of this aerial habitat that makes life easier for them than if they had to compete on the ground. Here the filmy ferns flourish; so do polypodies, spleenworts, the shoestring ferns, many clubmosses, and most of the innumerable species of the genus *Elaphoglossum*.

This tree trunk is coated with mosses, polypodies, and filmy ferns.

201

As we found out earlier, there are in fact a few epiphytes that can make it through a dry season, sometimes in near-desert situations with severe drought conditions. They're conditioned to areas only occasionally watered by rain, which quickly drains off or evaporates. From these groups come many of our successful house plants: the Boston fern, the bird's-nest fern, *Davallia, Humata,* some of the poly-podies, and the staghorns.

Some of these have developed special adaptations to cope with the lack of moisture and other survival problems. The shield leaves of the staghorns catch and store moisture and nutrients. Their old dead leaves form thick pads that act as sponges behind the plant. Some groups of epiphytes have acquired the peculiar ability to shear off, or drop, their own leaves cleanly. We don't yet understand what purpose this serves—it may help keep the plants free from disease—but *Humata, Davallia, Polypodium,* and their relatives can all do it, and it's certain that one day we'll figure out why. *Nephrolepis,* a relative of *Davallia,* has worked out a spe-cialty of its own: it doesn't drop leaves, but cuts off individ-ual pinnae.

Regarding light, ferns have a tolerance range that shows up in the tropical forests. Some can take the darkness of the overgrown forest floor, but even those that can are more abundant near clearings or where there are breaks in the canopy. For spore germination, light is absolutely necessary. Some species need less, some more, but almost no fern can get its start without some exposure to strong light. As the forest grows and darkens over the years, the ferns estab-lished there mature as the forest matures, adjusting and surviving in the curtailed light; what happens is that they have increasing difficulty in reproducing by spores. They have developed the vegetative methods of reproduction we have already examined, and propagate by buds, bulblets, roots, and so on, which do not depend on light.

The open areas of wet forests also have their special fern colonies, flourishing in full sun on road banks, in clearings, and in other exposed places that are not "typical" fern sites. Ferns comfortable here are the pantropic nodding clubmoss (*Lycopodium cernuum*), the silverbacks and goldbacks (*Pityrogramma*), and the strange forking *Gleichenias*, a large genus that, given half a chance, will proliferate into dense thickets that challenge even the aggressive bracken.

The higher the elevation, the cooler the temperature and

The polypodies constitute one of the most abundant epiphytic fern groups. Shown here is *Polypodium subpetiolatum*.

the heavier the moisture. These conditions combine to create the misty areas called cloud forests. Horticulturists working in temperate zones don't always realize that there are many tropical ferns that require low temperatures, but the cloud forests are full of ferns that have chosen, or adapted to, elevations of 8,000 to 10,000 feet, where it is not only always cool but occasionally below freezing. Cloud-forest ferns are often cold-loving relatives of the generally temperate *Dryopteris, Polystichum,* and *Athyrium;* we also find many species of *Polypodium, Grammitis,* and filmy ferns.

A few ferns in cloud forests have
a slime sheath on their fiddleheads and white
"aerophores" to obtain oxygen.

One particularly interesting adaptation in the cloud forests shows up in the crosiers of *Thelypteris* and *Blechnum:* a slimy covering decorated with white aerophores that stick out and act like snorkels. The slime sheath may have been produced by the fern as a protection, but it keeps out the oxygen required by the living tissues underneath it. To compensate, the plants improved the sheath with a breathing mechanism in the scalelike aerophores. These have abundant breathing pores, or stomata, at their tips, so that oxygen can be supplied to the underlying tissues.

On mountaintops along the Andean chain from Costa Rica south are the remote, exotic regions called paramos. These scrubby lands are cold, cloudy, wet, and full of special plants. Among them are the primordial-looking tree *Blechnums,* stout-trunked trees rising to 15 feet with stiff, leathery pinnate fronds. They resemble the cycads, which are a seed-plant group, and have been confused with them in the past, but they are ferns. Clubmosses abound here, too, in many forms; especially notable are the terrestrial *Lycopodium crassum* and *L. contiguum.* But the most distinctive of all is *Jamesonia,* the fern that never grows up. The slender leaves of *Jamesonia* never completely unroll their fronds. While the tip is very slowly unrolling, the lower pinnae have plenty of time to mature and drop their spores. In fact, the fronds finally die before the tip has managed to unroll all the way, so *Jamesonia* exists as a permanent crosier—a case of exceedingly slow development.

swamps, ponds, and water ferns

There are ferns that live around water and ferns that live in water. We find water babies of every gradation, from those that simply like their feet wet (on banks and in swamps) to

205

those that choose to be submerged, sometimes for part of the year, sometimes as their way of life.

Some of the more familiar temperate ferns are swamp-lovers. The sensitive fern, for example, which in spite of its name is one of the few that can take prolonged full sun, can almost always be found in places where it gets a combination of open space with wet marshy land. In such happy environments it takes hold and marches outward ruggedly, covering extensive patches with its branching, creeping rhizomes. There's nothing sensitive about it—until cold weather takes over. At the first frost we learn the reason for its name. It dies down dramatically, not merely turning brown, but wilting abruptly like a wrung-out dishrag.

Osmundas too are often near or in water. If there's a nearby swamp you can explore, check out any small hummocks or slightly raised areas: the showy cinnamon and the

This stand of tree ferns in southern Mexico is typical of wet mountainous areas in the tropics.

Jamesonia of the high mountains
of the Andes and Central America never
completes the unrolling of its fronds.

royal frequently choose such spots on which to establish themselves.

In tropical swamps we find *Blechnum serrulatum* (which, harsh though it sounds, really must be called a weed), *Thelypteris interrupta,* and the largest of all swamp ferns, the giant leather-leaf *(Acrostichum).* There are only three species of this curious genus, two of which grow in fresh water while the third, *A. aureum,* is the only fern known to prefer the salt of brackish water, flourishing in mangrove swamps. *Acrostichum* leaves are from 8 to 15 feet tall, pinnate, and distinctively thick-textured, with sporangia spread over the entire lower surface of the pinnae. The Malayan *Polypodium pteropus* and the Latin American *P. obtusifolium* and *P. rachypterygium* also have odd growth habits: they grow in streams with their small rhizomes so tightly bound around rocks that they cannot be extricated unless the rhizome is broken.

Truly aquatic ferns are often hard to recognize as ferns and equally often hard to classify. The water sprite (*Ceratopteris*) may root on muddy banks but often floats freely in water, becoming weedy in tropical ponds and slow-moving streams. Its much-branched fronds grow buds and young plantlets in the leaf notches, making it quite prolific, so it's a good plant for a fish tank that you want to fill rapidly with plantlets. However, it creates problems for botanists. So far as we know, it has only four species. The vegetative propagation makes it certain that the local populations will be much alike, so there's no trouble with those, but as it spreads over the wider areas of its range, things change. The variation becomes considerable, even significant. Are the variations merely varieties, or are they distinct species? On the other hand, are the four species we currently accept really distinct species? In short, how many *Ceratopteris* species are there? Botanical detective work is made of questions like these, and there are a lot of such questions—and not just about ferns.

The water clover *Marsilea* is one of those ferns so unfernlike in appearance that you simply have to accept the specialists' word that that's what it is. It may grow on muddy shores, but more often its creeping rhizomes root in mud under water, sending up leaves that look like four-leaved clovers to float on the surface. The rhizome has adapted to an underwater habitat by developing large air spaces in its outer cortex, by means of which oxygen is conveyed to the tissues of the stem. The spores of the water clover, like those of the other water ferns, are carried not on the leafy part of the front but in oval, nutlike sporocarps at the base of the leaf stalk. The sporangia within produce both male and female spores, and they are released into the water only as the sporocarps soften and rot open.

In addition to the sixty warm-area species of water clover, there are two related aquatic genera that show interesting leaf developments—in these cases, a series of reductions in leaf blades. *Regnellidium diphyllum* of Brazil has only two leaflets, and the six species of *Pilularia* (including *P. americana*, *P. globulifera*, and *P. minuta*) have no leaflets at all. The leaves are nothing more than naked leaf stalks. *Pilularia* looks like a grass, but on careful examination one can see the unrolling fiddleheads (actually the unrolling leaf stalks) and the sporocarps nestled among the leaf bases in the manner typical of water ferns.

There is also a fascinating group known as the floating ferns. The one called water spangles (*Salvinia*) grows so rapidly and thickly that it can cover a large water surface,

209

forming a mat that cuts off light and oxygen for other living organisms. Its oval leaves are covered with peculiar hairs, each actually a structure compounded of four hairs that are fused at the base and free toward the tip (in some species the tips re-fuse to form a small cage). These hairs keep water droplets off the leaves, which occur in pairs on the floating rhizome. Water spangles grows well in aquariums, but can be troublesome in the wild. At one time *S. auriculata,* having accidentally escaped from cultivation in Ceylon, was very soon clogging irrigation and drainage ditches and completely covering rice paddies, interfering seriously with cultivation of the essential rice. In Africa, two years after *S. molesta* was first observed in the lake behind the newly formed Kariba Dam, the plant had covered two hundred square miles of water.

The water spangles
(*Salvinia minima*) floats in the water and has
round leaves covered with hairs.

Another floating fern, the mosquito fern (*Azolla*), displays peculiarities of its own, but in this case the unique characteristics may turn out to be beneficial, particularly to the world food situation. In each of the mosquito fern's tiny (a thirty-second of an inch across) leaves is a small pouch that always contains the blue-green alga *Anabaena azollae*. We already know that many of the blue-green algae can convert nitrogen to a form more readily used by other plants, and it has lately been reported from Vietnam that where *Azolla pinnata* occurs in rice paddies, rice production is considerably increased. Experiments and tests are currently under way to determine if the mosquito fern's *Anabaena* is indeed the stimulating factor. If we find that it is, we may be able to use the knowledge to increase rice yields in other parts of the world.

The mosquito fern
(*Azolla filiculoides*) has overlapping leaves less than a sixteenth of an inch long.

dry and rocky places

From water, water, everywhere we leap over the intermediate environments to certain dry, rocky areas where—out of character though it may seem—some ferns do grow. These sites cannot be totally arid or perpetually dry; at some time there must be enough water for gametophyte development and for young sporophytes to become established. Given this minimum, pteridophytes will set themselves up near rocks. Rocks not only provide protection from sun and wind but also siphon moisture from deep in the soil to pass along to the plants, increasing their chances of hanging on to life. These rock ferns are generally related forms, the cheilanthoids, members of the genera *Cheilanthes, Notholaena,* and *Pellaea* and their close relatives.

We saw earlier that ferns only one cell thick need the highest possible humidity to survive, so it's logical that ferns struggling to adapt to dry air will develop leaves of especially thick texture. Some do, but more often they go even further, producing leaves that actually shrivel up, thus exposing less surface to the drying air and protecting the pores or stomata found on the lower surface. Many of these arid-area plants also have thicker cuticle covering the epidermis, an additional help in reducing water loss.

One of the most interesting of these plants is the resurrection plant (*Selaginella lepidophylla*). This spikemoss occurs from the southwestern United States across to southern Mexico, often choosing the driest areas where no other pteridophyte even tries to survive. When its soil is dry, the resurrection plant is a tight brown ball, but if soaked with water for a couple of hours it performs a miracle: it becomes what it really is, a widely spreading, flat, dark green rosette. The dry resurrection plants are often sold as novelties.

Top: Even in very dry regions there are
often a few ferns, such as *Cheilanthes myriophylla*,
nestled among the rocks. Bottom: The resurrection
plant appears as a brown ball in the dry season
but quickly unrolls when moisture is restored.

213

214

Cheilanthes sinuata is typical
of dry, rocky limestone regions of Mexico
and the southwestern United States.

Most ferns like their soil slightly acid, but there are a few that respond better when a bit of lime in the neighborhood makes the soil more alkaline. These lime-lovers often grow on or near limestone or other calcareous rocks. Limestone outcrops are widespread throughout the world, so the habitat is not a problem. Sometimes the area is small, sometimes not: the whole Caribbean basin is predominantly limy.

Most species of halberd ferns (*Tectaria*) and many maidenhairs (*Adiantum*) and spleenworts (*Asplenium*) live best on limestone rocks, but there are some species that have become very specific, choosing only *certain* rocks. *Cheilanthes siliquosa* is found only on serpentine rocks in western North America. *Phyllitis scolopendrium* is generally found in North America only on the Niagara escarpment of dolomitic limestone, although in Europe this fern spreads itself around much less selectively.

conservation: how and why

Some ferns are becoming extremely scarce in the wild, for a variety of reasons. Some grow too slowly, some produce few spores, some cannot compete well with other plants. Though we see the evidence, we haven't yet studied enough cases to understand all the cases of rarity.

There are some species in whose decline man clearly has had a hastening hand. It's not always a question of extensive collection. *Selaginella lepidophylla* is collected and sold as a novelty. *Dryopteris intermedia* and *Polystichum munitum* are cut for florists' arrangements. The root masses of the cinnamon and royal ferns are gathered to be sold as osmunda fiber, an excellent soil conditioner and rooting medium. In none of these cases do we find that the entire species is being threatened.

215

On the other hand, we have the case of the tree ferns, whose root masses have been used extensively as substrate for epiphytic plants. The root mantles of tree-fern trunks apparently do a better support job than osmunda: the material is firmer and can be cut into a variety of shapes. It is also more durable than osmunda, which starts to break down in a couple of years. The early surge of demand for tree-fern fiber led to a wholesale cutting of these plants in the tropics. Fortunately, no species is likely to become totally extinct, because most tree ferns become fertile, dropping spores and thus reproducing, before they are large enough to be harvested for their root mantle. But some of the species were certainly endangered; in some cases whole tree-fern forests have been reduced to a point where there are few good stands of particular species left. This greatly upsets the ecological balance of the area and puts the entire ecosystem into chaos, endangering species other than tree ferns. The trade in tree-fern trunks is now restricted by international laws, so perhaps the destructive process has been turned around in time.

Individual collectors are also a threat. These mild, plant-loving, life-loving citizens can raid the wilds as ruthlessly as Genghis Khans when they're after particular ferns for their gardens. The American hart's-tongue has been greatly diminished in its more accessible localities in New York State. In Vermont the green spleenwort has been almost entirely wiped out by collectors. These are only two examples among many, and the saddest aspect of the situation is that in almost every case the rare ferns (other than sterile hybrids) do far better when a grower takes the trouble to propagate them from spores than when he rips them up out of the wild and forces them into a new environment. All things being equal, spore-grown plants adapt far better than transplanted mature plants.

But the greatest danger to ferns is the one they share with all other plants—the rampant destruction of habitats in many parts of the world. There are examples right around us. The curly-grass fern (*Schizaea pusilla*), hard enough at best to find in the bogs of the northeastern United States, is becoming increasingly rare as housing developments lower the water table. There are plenty of other examples farther away. The rare and curious potato fern of Costa Rica (*Solanopteris brunei*) is among those on their way out as their sites are gradually destroyed.

In the tropics agriculture has virtually eliminated the natural vegetation in many areas. Fortunately, many lowland species are widespread and can survive in small patches of forest. This is not so true of middle-elevation montane forests, which are also being encroached on by the pressures of advancing population. Many epiphytic species can survive only on the well-established trees of a mature forest. One species of clubmoss has managed to establish itself in the disturbed habitat of cacao plantations, but it is the exception that points up the rule that most clubmosses will not survive when their mature host trees are cut down. Even the most selective lumbering inevitably does some damage, since it lets in so much unaccustomed light that many species cannot adjust to it and do not survive.

The danger exists. What can be done about it? We are certainly preserving plants in our botanical gardens around the world, but botanical gardens can hold only small samplings of individual species. What we really need to work toward is the preservation of whole ecosystems, with all their interdependencies in operation. Surely this is the best and

217

most effective means of preserving not only ferns but other plant groups: to protect habitat samples of significant size and diversity throughout the world. Perhaps, as the ecologists among us become increasingly vocal, even those who haven't given the problem much thought will gradually begin to see that the endangerment and despoilment must eventually affect us all.

There are also ways in which professionals might be more effective. It takes knowledge to care for rare ferns, and not many institutions have the staff or the time. For example, very few botanical gardens in the tropics have fern collections of significant size. Efforts must be made to obtain, propagate, and disseminate rare and endangered pteridophytes before they are lost. Information and plants should be exchanged among botanical centers. Real efforts should be made to introduce into general horticulture all those fern species that have not yet been tried and studied.

Another thing professionals can do is bring more amateurs into the act. As we've seen, spores can be sown at home. Tender ferns can be tested by any gardener interested enough to study up on the basics—in homes, small greenhouses, and other modified environments like those described earlier.

These efforts always result in pleasure and personal satisfaction, and sometimes in unexpected scientific gains. Mrs. Virginia Otto of Westboro, Massachusetts, recently produced from spores the rare Chinese *Asplenium delavayi*. On the basis of dried specimens, the only material previously available to them, some botanists had placed the plant in the Mexican genus *Schaffneria*. But with Mrs. Otto's living plant to study, I soon realized that *Schaffneria* and *A. delavayi* were not at all closely related. What Mrs. Otto had grown was a plant representing a whole new genus of ferns, which I have called *Sinephropteris*.

The invaluable Mrs. Otto, who is just the sort of amateur we need, has also been instrumental in preserving another species, not only rare but endangered. From spores she obtained from a *Diplazium laffanianum* in the Bermuda Botanical Garden, she successfully grew several of these plants. When she started them, she knew that the plant grew only on Bermuda, and that it was no longer showing up in its usual localities, most of them having been destroyed by human encroachment. What the authorities in Bermuda tell us now is that the plant is actually extinct in the wild, the only ones left on the whole island being the four preserved in their Garden. But Mrs. Otto, bless her, now has eight, and we at the New York Botanical Garden have four, which she gave to us. Eventually it will be propagated more extensively and reestablished in natural habitats on Bermuda, and humankind will have repaired some of the damage it has done.

With a little patience, anyone who cares about ferns can grow them from spores. It's probably one of the best ways to save rare and endangered species, since—as I pointed out in Chapter 4—spores can be so easily distributed and exchanged. Why not experiment with it, and find out if this way of increasing your fern garden is the right one for you?

9.

field trips and forays

ow, primed with information and presumably full of enthusiasm, you've decided that a fern garden, indoors or out, is what you're going to have. What's the best way to go about it?

The obvious first step is to descend on a nearby dime store, or better yet a good local nursery, find a fern that appeals to you, take it home, and see how you both make out. If you've already done this and are encouraged, investigate the mail-order nursery scene. Several very good mail-order nurseries specialize in native ferns. Many others offer a good selection of tender ferns, ranging from common natives to some very rare, exotic species.

Alternatively, or perhaps at the same time, get in touch with a botanical garden in your area. You will see their ferns growing and probably learn about good candidates not otherwise available to you, and they often have extra plants for sale. If you spend enough time around the fern areas, you'll also probably get into conversations with fern specialists of every degree, and since most enthusiasts are more than eager to share their expertise with interested novices, you'll pick up invaluable hints just by asking a few questions.

But probably the best step you can take is to put yourself in touch with other fern people. The American Fern Society is only one of several around the world (see pages 228 – 29). Some are local, with specialized material; some are international. The members are both amateur and professional, and the professional growers can open up great new vistas of commercial availability. The amateurs may be no less useful, with interesting plants and all kinds of practical wisdom to share. You'll be able to exchange plant divisions or even whole plants. Innumerable raffles, sales, and publications will enrich your involvement. Fern societies sponsor trips to gardens, nurseries, private collections, and wild areas—places you might otherwise have trouble getting to or not even know about. Society meetings are another important activity, particularly when they put you in touch with members from other parts of the world. This personal contact is the best way to exchange information.

One of the best things a fern society can do for you is to make it easier to grow ferns from spores. Several societies maintain spore banks that members can draw on at nominal cost, usually twenty-five to fifty cents per packet. The largest is at the American Fern Society, whose bank contains more than eight hundred kinds of fern spores donated by members and botanical gardens from around the world. Neill Hall, the spore bank's director, logs in this often exotic material, divides it into resalable small packets (containing enough for one to several pots of prothalli), and stores them in the refrigerator. As requests come in, he fills them from his stockpile, cool, fresh, and ready to go. Mr. Hall is a shining example, or perhaps a cautionary one, of the dedicated fern enthusiast. Organizing, recording, and disseminating (there are more than five thousand requests per year) obviously add up to a full-time job, and he has done it for more than fifteen years on a volunteer basis.

Apart from the expanded horizons that can come to you through a fern society, how about what you can do for yourself when you're traveling? Spores, especially, are very easy to transport. All you need is a supply of envelopes that can be sealed, or even plain paper that can be folded into packets and sealed with tape. Break or cut off from an interesting plant a piece that bears mature spores, and slip it into one of your packets. Dampness will create mold, so if there's any chance that your specimens are even slightly damp, put the packets between paper for a couple of days to draw off moisture. It's perfectly legal to bring these packets into the United States, and customs officials should give you no trouble.

If you want to bring whole plants in from foreign countries, things get a bit more complicated. There are two essential bases to cover for a start. First, before you leave the United States, get from the Department of Agriculture a list of the regulations governing this kind of traffic. Generally, for the United States, ferns other than tree ferns may come in as long as their roots are completely soil-free and they have no known disease or insect infestation. You will need an import permit, which is easily obtained from the Department of Agriculture Permit Unit, Room 638, Federal Building, PPQ, APHIS, U.S. Department of Agriculture, Hyattsville, Maryland 20782. Second, find out from local authorities in the country you're visiting what their regulations are on plants that may and may not be dug up, and may or may not be taken out of the country.

Having thus prepared yourself, you can have a fern-collecting field day, particularly if you're lucky enough to be traveling in the tropics. Even without expert guidance, you're sure to encounter many species so common and conspicuous that they cannot be missed. Finding forty species at one site is not unusual; I have sometimes found as many as a hundred. The roadside weeds pioneering on exposed banks, impossible to overlook, are well worth digging up. The *Pityrogrammas* and maidenhairs that grow this way are especially attractive and transplant easily.

224

Caution: don't wade in and dig up everything you see. Nothing gives plant collecting a worse name than the undisciplined raiders who greedily cram their boxes and suitcases with every living plant in sight. Choose only from abundant species, and then dig up only a selected few. You should take only what you can realistically transport and care for.

Dig up your specimens carefully, disturbing the roots as little as possible. Wash them clean, removing all dirt from the roots. Remove any damaged or suspect-looking leaves. *Note the habitat!* Do it with photographs: pictures of how and where the plant grows and what surrounds its growing area can be invaluable. Do it with notes: put down every possible detail of temperature, exposure, soil, rocks, any physical aspect that seems pertinent, so that you can adjust conditions to the best of your ability when you get your plant home.

After the plants have been cleaned and the excess water has been drained off, place them in plastic bags to keep them from drying out. Before packing them for your journey home, remove a few perfectly good leaves. It seems brutal, but too many leaves add to the difficulties of transporting and transplanting. They make the plant more bulky and provide too much surface for water loss, something the plant cannot afford until its roots, reestablished in its new home, are once again strongly drawing moisture from the soil. If there are handsome large leaves you can't bear to remove, cut them in half. It won't hurt the plant, and the leaves will be able to continue their food-producing function, so you'll feel better about the whole thing.

It's also handy, at times, to collect dried specimens rather than living plants. You can't plant them, but they can be

226

Fern collectors will
find good use for plastic bags
in wet tropical forests.

used in arrangements, as study specimens, for crafts projects, and so on. You can dry plants very simply by smoothing them flat between sheets of newspaper (which is highly absorbent), fortifying the newspapers with corrugated cardboard or blotters, then placing the whole arrangement under some sort of weight or pressure. You can use a large, heavy book, or you can make something more elaborate— a plant press. Alternate corrugated cardboards and folded newspapers, with the plant specimens inside the newspapers. With a board at top and bottom, tie the whole thing firmly together with ropes or straps. Drying is accelerated if such a press is placed over mild heat in such a way that the channels of cardboard carry off the moisture. I've done this with lanterns, camp stoves, even electric light bulbs, but a

Specimens for study are often dried
in a plant press, composed of sheets of newspaper
between corrugated cardboards.

227

moving car in good weather can be just as effective. Tie the press atop the car roof so that the channels of the corrugated boards face into the wind, and take off. You'll probably be able to devise even more ways for yourself if you keep in mind that the object of the process is very simple: to remove moisture from the plants without wrinkling or breaking them.

Again, remember to make labels. Include locality, species name, habitat description, collector, and date.

fern societies

The American Fern Society (c/o Department of Botany, Smithsonian Institution, Washington, D.C. 20560), an international organization of amateurs and professionals, was founded in 1893. It publishes the quarterly *American Fern Journal*, the bimonthly bulletin *Fiddlehead Forum*, and *Pteridologia*, a series of memoirs of long botanical papers. In addition to an annual organization-wide meeting and field trip, the local chapters hold monthly meetings, with field trips, shows, and other activities.

The Los Angeles International Fern Society (4369 Tujunga Avenue, North Hollywood, California 91604) puts out a monthly bulletin along with a two-page lesson sheet on how to grow different species. It holds monthly meetings in the Los Angeles area and has members around the world.

Florida is a major center for fern activities. Several societies there hold regular monthly meetings and offer a choice of field trips and other activities. The oldest of these, the South Florida Fern Society (P.O. Box 55-7275, Ludlam Branch, Miami, Florida 33155), publishes the monthly *Florida Fern Notes* and puts on an annual fern festival in cooperation with the Fairchild Tropical Garden. The International Tropical Fern Society (8720 Southwest 34th Street, Miami, Florida 33165) is another group with several chapters, mostly in the southeastern region. It publishes the monthly *Rhizome Reporter.*

Other fern societies operate in Philadelphia (the Delaware Valley Fern Society), Memphis, and Houston. The Northwest Ornamental Horticultural Society sponsors a fern study group centered in Bellevue, Washington, near Seattle. The British Pteridological Society (c/o Lt. Col. Philip G. Coke, Robin Hill, Stinchcombe, Dursley, Gloucestershire, England) holds monthly meetings and offers its members a very well-organized program of field trips throughout Great Britain. It also puts out two annual publications, the *Fern Gazette* and the *Bulletin.*

In Continental Europe the Schweizerische Vereinigung der Farnfreunde (Swiss Association of Fern Friends) has recently been organized. If they are true to their name, you can make contact here with friendly fellow amateurs interested in field botany and fern gardening.

Elsewhere in the world are the Japanese Pteridological Society and the Nippon Fernist Club in Japan; the Nelson New Zealand Fern Society in New Zealand; and the fern study group of the Society for Growing Australian Plants in Australia. An international organization of professional pteridologists has also been created to stimulate communication among researchers.

10.

ferns around the world

before your own garden has had time to become the green paradise of your vision, it might be a good idea to tour around looking at what professionals have done in the way of design and display with their fern collections. The list that follows describes only a sampling of fern areas open to the public. There are many more, and there are also state and local parks that feature fern walks. Investigate those you can. You'll see some stunning vistas, some outstanding individual plants, some impressive collections, and you'll learn a great deal about ferns that can't be picked up from books.

public fern displays
United States

Bartholomew's Cobble, Sheffield, Massachusetts. In the shaded mossy limestone outcrops and moist woods of this preserve along the Housatonic River, many ferns are at home: several spleenworts, the walking fern, common species of wood ferns, and a number of their hybrids.

New York Botanical Garden, Bronx, New York. The Fern Gallery in the Conservatory displays the largest selection of ferns under glass in the United States. More than four hundred kinds are planted around a spectacular waterfall and pool, and visitors look down on this fern forest from a skywalk. There are additional selections of native and other hardy ferns in a native plant garden and a rock garden.

Cary Arboretum, Millbrook, New York. This is the arboretum of the New York Botanical Garden. Many native

The Fern Gallery at the newly
restored Enid Haupt Conservatory of
the New York Botanical Garden.

ferns, as well as hardy ferns from temperate regions around the world, are settled in its Fern Glen. The visitor sees them in these natural settings as he or she walks down woodland trails and crosses a boardwalk over a swamp. Lime-loving plants grow on limestone rocks, water ferns in a small pond. Many species are the products of spore-reproduction activity in the arboretum's greenhouse.

Brooklyn Botanic Garden, Brooklyn, New York. The conservatory houses a small but very interesting collection of ferns, with epiphytes particularly well displayed on a simulated oak tree. Native ferns are planted outdoors.

Morris Arboretum, Philadelphia, Pennsylvania. The Fernery is a tiny gem of a fern house, the only public greenhouse of this arboretum. Narrow paths wind among excellent rockwork, and from them one sees some exceptional specimens: a walking holly fern, many tree ferns, a very large felt fern, and as a bonus a waterfall decorated with an abundant growth of filmy ferns.

Longwood Garden, Kennett Square, Pennsylvania. In this outstanding complex of public gardens, the Fern Passage makes a particularly lush display with many immaculately cultivated tender ferns. Noteworthy are the pendent clubmosses, the very large staghorn *Platycerium superbum*, the large and fleshy *Marattia lygodiifolia*, the sensational *Davallia* basket mentioned in Chapter 6, tree ferns, maidenhairs, and many, many others. Hardy ferns are planted outdoors along a woodland trail.

United States National Arboretum, Washington, D.C. Fern Valley was established here in 1953. On an easy trail along a shaded stream, there is a good representation of native American ferns. Hardy foreign ferns are planted in a separate garden.

Ferny rockwork at Garfield Park, Chicago.

Fairchild Tropical Garden, Coral Gables, Florida. The large Rare Plant House contains a good number of tropical ferns, including maidenhairs and tree ferns.

Fernwood, Niles, Michigan. Naturalized fern plantings on the grounds of Mrs. Kay Boydston, along with many flowers and shrubs, became the nucleus of the present nature and crafts center on the Boydston property. More than one hundred thirty kinds of hardy ferns are planted along the trails and in the rock garden.

Garfield Park, Chicago, Illinois. This city park has one of the world's most impressive fern houses. It does not contain a great variety of species, but all are wonderfully displayed on excellent rockwork, which rises steeply from the path so that the ferns can be seen at close range in the rock crevices. Fernlike cycads, a waterfall, and a large pool help to create a completely convincing atmosphere, as do beds of *Selaginella martensii* and rows of the small tree fern *Blechnum gibbum*.

Golden Gate Park, San Francisco, California. This beautiful park is distinctive because it represents the most northerly site at which tree ferns have been planted outdoors in North America. In its attractive wooded setting eight species are flourishing, including *Cyathea medullaris* and three species of *Dicksonia*. *Hypolepis rugulosa* and several other tropical and south-temperate ferns are succeeding here as well. A greenhouse complex houses many more ferns, and there are also well-cared-for flower gardens.

Muir Woods, seventeen miles north of San Francisco, California. This rich redwood forest is an excellent place for viewing an abundance of native ferns: lady fern, western sword fern, several polypodies, the giant chain fern, the giant horsetail, and many others.

University of California, Berkeley, California. Outdoors, in a wooded setting, there is a good planting of native ferns. The greenhouse contains several hundred additional species from all parts of the world.

Ferndell, Griffith Park, Los Angeles, California. In this wooded area numerous tree ferns, staghorns, and other exotic specimens are planted in a natural setting along a stream, where there are also masses of *Microlepia strigosa*. Trails and waterfalls make the area especially attractive.

Los Angeles State and County Arboretum, Arcadia, California. At present the fern collection is contained in one fern house and scattered throughout other greenhouses. An outdoor fern grotto is under development.

Tree-fern forest in Golden Gate Park, San Francisco.

237

Hawaii National Park, Hawaii. Ferns naturally abound on several of the islands, and the lush growth here is truly spectacular. There is a broad sampling of the rich native fern flora, with tree ferns and *Gleichenias* being especially notable.

Canada
Montreal Botanical Garden, Montreal, Quebec. A fine selection of tender ferns is attractively displayed in the conservatory's fern house.

Puerto Rico
Luquillo National Forest, El Yunque. This cloud-covered mountain twenty miles east of San Juan is rich in tree ferns, filmy ferns, and other groups typical of tropical wet forests. Roads and attractive trails make all parts of the mountain readily accessible.

West Indies
While there are a few ferns in the hot lowlands, most of the rich fern areas of these islands are in the wet mountains, those high enough to catch abundant rainfall. Fern-lovers therefore should investigate the mountains of Hispaniola, Jamaica, Cuba, and some in the Lesser Antilles, like Dominica and Grenada.

Mexico
University of Mexico, Mexico City. In the Invernadero, a domed greenhouse, a good variety of tropical ferns is collected. Attractive display use is made of the local lava rock, formed into rock steps and grottoes in whose crevices young ferns flourish, enjoying their natural background.

Costa Rica

Much of this country can be considered a large botanical garden. Many roadsides are covered with ferns, and especially ferny areas are easily reached by automobile. Volcán Poás National Park, one of the richer sites, contains more than a hundred species. The Pan American Highway south of San Jose passes over the high Talamanca Mountains, including the Cerro de la Muerte, which was once covered with rich wet oak forests. Unfortunately, these forests are now being cut down, but some patches are left. Of special interest near the top are the areas of paramo with the curious *Jamesonia*, species of terrestrial clubmosses, and tree *Blechnums* close to the road.

Brazil

Rio de Janeiro Botanical Garden. This lovely park has many ferns scattered throughout. Organ Mountains Park, just outside Rio, has an abundance of native ferns.

Great Britain

Royal Botanic Gardens at Kew, Richmond, Surrey, England. Three greenhouses here—a large tropical fern house, a cool fern house, and a filmy fern house—hold the largest indoor fern collection in the world. The diversity of the species gathered here is impressive. Visitors view the filmy ferns through a large glass wall behind which the ferns are set against a rock wall along with *Dicksonia* tree ferns.
Royal Botanic Garden, Edinburgh, Scotland. The large new greenhouse complex here contains a sizable fern house that holds a most impressive *Dicksonia* tree-fern forest. Other ferns are planted among the *Dicksonias*, some even growing on their trunks.

239

240

Part of the extensive fern
collection in the tropical house at the Royal
Botanic Garden at Kew, England.

A forest of New Zealand tree ferns
highlights the fern house of the Royal Botanic
Garden, Edinburgh, Scotland.

241

West Germany
Botanical Garden, Berlin-Dahlem. The fern house contains a good selection of tropical ferns, and there is also a good variety in the larger palm house, where rockwork and waterfalls add to the pleasure of viewing tree ferns, masses of *Selaginella martensii*, and large specimens of bird's-nest ferns.

Munich Botanical Garden. Here, both in the fern house and in the larger palm house, one will find perhaps the finest fern collection in Continental Europe. Native and other hardy ferns can also be seen in the *Farnschlucht*, an outdoor fern gorge.

Soviet Union
Komarov Botanical Institute, Leningrad. The fern house, part of the large conservatory complex, contains a fair assemblage of ferns.

South Africa
National Botanic Garden, Kirstenbosch, near Cape Town. Tree ferns and other species are naturalized along streams and ponds here.

India
National Botanic Garden, Lucknow. This garden has a good collection of ferns, particularly varieties native to the Himalayas and peninsular India.

Singapore
Singapore Botanical Garden. The efforts of a succession of outstanding directors have made this one of the most splendid botanical gardens in the world. Even while the

A fern wall and waterfall
in the palm house at the Botanical
Garden, Berlin-Dahlem, Germany.

243

Japanese occupied the area during World War II, the director, R. E. Holttum, was permitted to continue his work on orchids and ferns. This area of the world is one of the richest in ferns, and the gardens contain a good representation of native species. Seeing large epiphytic ferns such as the bird's-nest and several staghorns outdoors in their natural setting is a thrilling experience.

Indonesia
Bogor Botanic Garden, Java. One of the finest collections of native ferns in Southeast Asia can be seen here and at the garden at Tjibodas, which includes a tree-fern grove.

Australia
Royal Botanic Gardens in South Yarra, Melbourne. Tree ferns and smaller ferns flourish in the shade of taller trees along a small stream here.

Native tree ferns can also be seen at Maguerie Pass, south of Sydney, as well as in the gorges of the Dandenong Hills near Melbourne. Roadsides throughout New South Wales and Victoria, especially in the Blue Mountains, are lined with these ferns.

New Zealand
Pukekura Park, New Plymouth, North Island. This park has one of the most interesting fern collections in the world. Some varieties are housed in its fernery, but there are also outstanding specimens of tree ferns throughout the park. In addition, the conservatories are connected by tunnels that are alive with ferns.

Mount Egmont, only a short distance from New Plymouth, offers the visitor a chance to see many of New Zealand's two hundred species of ferns growing in their natural habitat. And all the national parks on both of New Zealand's islands contain a rich sampling of native ferns.

fern shows and festivals

Many fern societies and horticultural organizations hold annual shows or festivals. These shows provide an exceptional opportunity for veteran fern fanciers as well as enthusiastic novices to see the best efforts of their fellow growers, to meet and exchange ideas with some of the most knowledgeable and dedicated people in the field, and to learn about the latest developments in fern cultivation. The following is a brief list of some of the larger shows. To find out about others, contact the fern society or botanical garden in your area.

New York

In late spring, the New York Chapter of the American Fern Society holds its annual Fern Festival at the New York Botanical Garden. There are displays, sales, demonstrations, and lectures.

Pennsylvania

The Delaware Valley Fern Society presents a Fern Festival each October at the Morris Arboretum in Philadelphia. Among the features are plant sales, displays, tours, and workshops.

Tennessee

Each spring, there is a day-long series of lectures and demonstrations presented at the Goldsmith Civic Garden Center by the Memphis Fern Society.

245

Washington

Every June in Seattle, the Northwest Ornamental Horticultural Society holds its grand sale for the benefit of the University of Washington Arboretum. A multitude of plants are offered, including many ferns.

California

The Los Angeles International Fern Society holds its Fern and Exotic Plant Show in late July. In addition to a large exhibition of commercial and private displays, there are demonstrations, slide shows, guided tours, and sales.

Florida

The annual fern show of the South Florida Fern Society takes place at the Fairchild Tropical Garden, Coral Gables, in May. The show is accompanied by sales, lectures, and greenhouse tours.

Puerto Rico

Tropiflora, a splendid exhibit held at the Coliseo Roberto Clemente in San Juan, is presented in April by the Puerto Rican Horticultural Society. The show features the wealth of native plants on the island, including many ferns. Attendance is usually over thirty thousand.

England

The Southport Flower Show offers a good selection of the best varieties of hardy ferns in displays presented by members of the British Pteridological Society. The Chelsea Flower Show also features good fern displays.

I'm certainly in favor of encouraging all gardeners to

plant ferns. I would particularly like to see them doing it from spores for the reasons I've emphasized throughout this book. But it's evident from the above lists, and from the prevalence of ferns throughout the world, that one doesn't even have to cultivate them to enjoy them. Invest a bit of time in learning something about them, keep your eyes open as you move around—even close to home—and you'll find ferns springing out at you from stone walls, from empty lots, from ditches. When you travel, your fern-wise eyes will discern things even more exciting. Watch road-banks, study hedges, tramp through woods. By all means see what you can of the "tamed" ferns on our list, but you'll find that seeing them in the wild is another kind of experience entirely. In fact, it has probably already occurred to you that a fern hobby can provide you with an excuse for

In many tropical regions the roadsides are covered with ferns.

247

traveling. Isn't a bona-fide fern-lover entitled to a personal look at the cloud forests of the Andes?

However, if circumstances keep you close to home, all is very far from lost. One of the best and most direct ways to get deeply into fern lore is to associate yourself with one of the botanical gardens in your area. Many gardens, trying to get along on generally skimpy budgets, are eager for volunteer help and rely on it heavily. Your time and work will be richly rewarded: you will inevitably learn from the contact with professionals, you will work with a great diversity of plants, you will find out what's new and what's best on the horticultural scene, and you'll get an opportunity to find out what goes on behind the scenes—even to see many plants not on view to the public. All this, of course, is repayment enough, but it also happens from time to time that devoted volunteers get to take home some of the garden's extra plants to enrich and enhance their own gardens. Your commitment to ferns, and to public service, may be very deep—but this is a little something extra to keep in mind.

appendix:
how ferns are classified

As I said on page 11, ferns are not classified by the way they look. How, then, do we classify them? With difficulty, with controversy, and even—it must be admitted—with occasional revision as increasingly sophisticated techniques give us new evidence.

The external form of a fern is certainly among the characteristics we consider. But we go far beyond form into internal anatomy, the arrangement and character of the vascular bundles, the venation patterns, the chromosome numbers, the hairs and scales, the habitat, the rhizome patterns, the cell patterns of the epidermis. Matching, tracing, and evaluating all of these elements guides our thinking.

But by far the most conclusive and reliable evidence of family membership comes to us through the sori, sporangia, and spores—the fertile areas of the plant. This is because the fertile parts of plants appear to be the most conservative, that is, the parts least likely to have changed over the centuries. Because they are exposed to the environment only briefly during the plant's life, they are protected, relatively unaffected by environment. The chances are good, therefore, that they most closely reflect their early ancestral structure. The vegetative plant parts—leaves, rhizomes, and so on—are much more constantly exposed, thus more likely to be affected by environment and changed over the long evolutionary period.

249

As an example of how our increasingly subtle botanical techniques often create confusion as they take us—we hope—toward eventual clarification, consider the annulus. A very important part of the fertile system, this is the specialized patch or row of thickened cells on the sporangium that must contract to open the sporangium and release spores into the air. Analysis of the characteristic forms of the annulus helped place a large group of ferns in the huge Polypodiaceae family. During the last forty years, however, botanists have come to realize that there are so many differences within the group that they probably represent several distinct families.

So far, so good, but this opens up another typical area of contention. How many distinct families? Some say three or four; some say as many as thirty-five. This is because some botanists are "splitters," making hairline divisions between genera and families, while others are "lumpers," willing to use much broader guidelines. Since there is no rule to dictate the limits of the size of a plant family, what we're left with is a matter of opinion, the opinion of scientific factions that cannot as yet come to a uniform conclusion even though they are equally qualified and all are considering the same evidence.

It's understandably difficult for the amateur to see how there can be such diversity of scientific opinion. But it exists, and it means for the moment that we really cannot say with authority that X number of ferns belong to the Y family, or that there are without question Z number of plant families. Neither the splitters nor the lumpers are to be considered unquestionably right or wrong. Both are, in their way, correct, but each group is using names of different levels to classify the same plants.

picture credits

Chapter 1
11, 13: JM; 14: Charles Neidorf; 19: NYBG; 23: Manabu Saito; 24: (top) Author's collection, (btm) NYBG.

Chapter 2
29 (top & btm), 31: JM; 34, 35: Engler & Prantl; 38, 39: JM; 41: Engler & Prantl; 44, 45: JM; 47: From W. H. Wagner, Jr., "Paraphyses: Filicineae," *Taxon* 13:2, 1964 (NYBG Library); 49, 50, 51, 52: Charles Neidorf; 55: NYBG; 56: Engler & Prantl; 57, 58: JM; 59: María Lebrón-Luteyn; 60, 61, 62: JM; 63, 66: NYBG.

Chapter 3
71: NYBG; 73: From A. L. A. Fée, *Genera Filicum,* Strasbourg & Paris, 1850–52 (NYBG Library); 74, 75, 80: Drawings by Edgar M. Paulton.

Chapter 4
87: JM; 93 (top & btm), 96, 98 (top & btm): AS.

Chapter 5
103, 104 (top & btm): AS; 105, 106, 107: JM; 108: AS; 110 (top & btm), 111: C. E. Delchamps; 112:

Engler & Prantl—From A. Engler and K. Prantl, *Die Natürlichen Pflanzenfamilien,* Vol. 1, Berlin, 1898–1900 (Courtesy New York Botanical Garden Library)

Engler & Prantl; 113: C. E. Delchamps.

Chapter 6
119: Thomas H. Everett; 122, 125 (top & btm), 128 (top & btm): AS; 131: (top) JM, (btm) F. G. Foster; 134, 139 (top & btm): AS; 145: (all) JM.

Chapter 7
162, 163: JM; 165: NYBG; 173: F. G. Foster; 174: JM; 175: (top) Courtesy American Fern Society, (btm) JM; 177, 178, 179, 182, 183: JM.

Chapter 8
189, 191: NYBG; 192: Engler & Prantl; 195: JM; 196: Dr. William Steere; 197: NYBG; 199: Courtesy American Fern Society; 201, 203, 204, 206, 207: JM; 210, 211: C. E. Delchamps; 213 (top & btm), 214: JM.

Chapter 9
226, 227: JM.

Chapter 10
233: AS; 235, 237, 240, 241, 243, 247: JM.

251

index

Boldface
numbers refer to
illustrations

A

Acrostichum aureum, 190, 208
adder's-tongue fern, 16, 32, 53, **107**
Adiantum, 198, 215
  capillus-veneris, 190
  caudatum, 111
  hispidulum, 138
  pedatum, 21, **163**, 164; var. minor,
  177
  raddianum, **145**
  reniforme, 33
  venustum, 164
aerophore, **204**, 205
air-layering, 105
algae, 97–99
Anemia, 44, 55–56, 193–94
  makrinii, 48
  oblongifolia, 20
  phyllitidis, **192**
Angiopteris evecta, 161
annulus, **73**, 74
antheridium, **75**, 76
apogamy, 79
apospory, 81
aquatic ferns, 208–11
archegonium, **75**,76
asparagus fern, 11
Asplenium, 81, 156, 176, 215
  bulbiferum, 109
  conquisitum, 137
  cuspidatum, **104**
  daucifolium, 109
  delavayi, 216
  exiguum, 113, 137, 157
  nidus, 130
  platyneuron, **80**, 137
  ruta-muraria, 138, 177
  trichomanes, 137, **175**
Asplenosorus ebenoides, **80**
Athyrium, 198
  filix-femina, **162**, 163
  filix-mas var. minutissimum, 177

niponicum cv. Pictum, 48, 164
  thelypterioides, **51**
autumn fern, 164
Azolla, 78
  filiculoides, **211**

B

bird's-nest fern, 48, 130, **131**, 202, 244
bladder-fern, 109, 176
Blechnum, 46, 105, 205
  ensiforme, 30
  fragile, 30
  gibbum, 236
  penna-marina, 177, 190–93
  serrulatum, 208
  spicant, **178**
Boston fern, 106, **119**, 120, 121–23,
  125, 202
Botrychium, 53
  lunaria, **197**
bottle garden, 138–40
bracken, 17–18, **19**, 21, 22, 28, **52**,
  180, 190, 200
brake
  Asian, 132–33
  Cretan, 79, 132
  spider, 133
  Victorian, 133, **145**
bramble fern, **29**
buckler fern, 163
bulblet bladder-fern, 109
button fern, **131**, 132

C

Camptosorus rhizophyllus, **80**, 138,
  175, 176
Ceratopteris, 76, 208–09
  thalictroides, 190
Ceterach, 177
chain fern, 173, 176
  European, 114
  giant, 164
  Oriental, 109
Cheilanthes, 45, 46, 176, 212
  myriophylla, **213**
  siliquosa, 215
  sinuata, **214**
Chinese kidney fern, 33
Christmas fern, **50**, 163, 180, 181
Cibotium barometz, 17
cinnamon fern, 53, 173, 181, **182**, 215